The Mind and Spirit of JOHN PETER ALTGELD

The Mind
and Spirit of
John Peter Altgeld

Selected Writings and Addresses
edited by Henry M. Christman

Essay Index Reprint Series

BOOKS FOR LIBRARIES PRESS
FREEPORT, NEW YORK

INTERNATIONAL STANDARD BOOK NUMBER:

0-8369-1860-6

LIBRARY OF CONGRESS CATALOG CARD NUMBER:

70-128200

PRINTED IN THE UNITED STATES OF AMERICA

contents

editor's preface

In problems and in atmosphere, the United States at the closing of the nineteenth century had a certain resemblance to the United States of today. The old America, symbolized by the yeoman farmer sturdy in his independence and individualism, had passed away forever. The Industrial Revolution had done its work. North and South, East and West, all Americans were caught up in the convulsions of the new industrial society.

Urban America was expanding at an amazing rate. In 1880, for instance, Chicago had a population of one-half million; in 1890, one million; in 1900, one and a half million; and by 1910, two million. Whole new cities were being created by the influx of impoverished families from rural America and from the distant lands of Europe. Housing, social services, urban decay, all the problems of the modern city, had become a concern to plague Americans from that day to this.

Nor were those who remained on the farm absolved from new problems. The farm was no longer an independent economic unit; henceforth, the farmer's life was to revolve around economic factors over which he had little or no control. What prices would his crops and livestock bring on the market when they arrived in a distant city? How much of his profit, if any, would remain after paying the railroad charges? What kind of interest rates would he have to pay in order to finance next year's crops?

All Americans suddenly found themselves completely dependent on a new economy which few understood. For better or for worse, the prosperity of the United States and all its citizens rested upon the vagaries of an industrial capitalism and its alternating cycles of inflation and depression.

Such was the picture which confronted John Peter Altgeld as events brought him forward as a leader in Illinois and the nation.

John Peter Altgeld, American reformer, jurist, and Governor of Illinois, was born in Nieder Selter, Germany, on December 30, 1847. When three months old, he was brought to the United States by his parents. The Altgelds settled on a farm near Mansfield, Ohio, where young John Peter was required at an early age to assume a major share of the burden of work.

The young Altgeld grew up in poverty, without formal schooling, living constantly in the shadow of a crude, stern, bigoted father whose provincial outlook contemplated no other future. John Peter was restive, and at age sixteen he enlisted in the Ohio Home Guards and served for one hundred days. His time away from home in military service provided the occasion for his complete rebellion against family parochialism. Mustered out of service, he refused to return to the old life of farm laborer and insisted on going ahead to secondary school. He proved so able at his studies that in a few years he was teaching school himself. After two years of teaching in the Mansfield vicinity, he left his boyhood home altogether to seek a new life in the West.

Working his way along as a farmhand, Altgeld reached Missouri, and eventually was forced by hardship to become a railroad laborer in Arkansas. Worse still, his military experience had left him with more than a yen to see new places; while in service, he had contracted a fever which was to recur again and again throughout future years. It now struck with particular severity and almost cost him his life. Ill, friendless, completely without funds, he made his way back to Missouri and reached the town of Savannah, where he was given the opportunity to resume schoolteaching.

The Savannah interlude was to be a turning point in Altgeld's life. Not only was he once again able to exercise his talents as a teacher, but he could spend his spare time studying law. In 1871, at the age of twenty-four, he was admitted to the bar; and in 1872 he became city attorney of Savannah, the northwestern Missouri town that was now his home. His growing prowess gave promise of the Altgeld to be. He extended his influence to the surrounding countryside, and, by defeating the political aspirations of a former mayor of Savannah, was elected in 1874 as county attorney of Andrew County, Missouri, on a coalition Democratic and Granger ticket.

The pattern was set; Altgeld had proven himself as lawyer and politician. He had found an ideological home in the Democratic-Granger political milieu and its exposition of Jeffersonianism. He was rapidly tiring of the burdens of a public prosecutor, and he considered himself ready for bigger things. In 1875 he submitted his resignation as county attorney, raised one hundred dollars, and made his way to Chicago.

Altgeld's first year in Chicago was a lean one; to save money, he lived in his little law office. And his responsibilities were to increase. During his second year in Chicago he married the sweetheart of his early youth, Emma Ford, who he had first met as a fellow schoolteacher in Ohio. But, after the early years, the Altgelds prospered. Altgeld carefully saved as much as possible from his legal fees and invested in real estate. His success was phenomenal. In 1879 he owned $500 worth of Chicago land; in just a few years he was negotiating real estate transactions involving hundreds of thousands of dollars. His first efforts had centered on the development of residential areas, but it was not long until he had holdings of business property in the heart of commercial Chicago. He became a builder; one office structure rose after another, Altgeld buildings on Altgeld property, all monuments to his growing affluence and power.

But Altgeld had not forgotten his impoverished background— or the Jeffersonian sentiments he had expounded in his rousing addresses before Missouri Grangers—or the gnawing doubts about law and justice which had haunted him as a Missouri prosecutor and a Chicago attorney. In 1884 he published his first book, *Our Penal Machinery and Its Victims*, in which he vigorously scored the entire system of law enforcement and prosecution.

In a few words, Altgeld summed up his reasons for condemning the whole penal system: "For it seems, first, to make criminals out of many that are not naturally so; and, second, to render it difficult for those convicted ever to be anything else than criminals; and, third, to fail to repress those that do not want to be anything but criminals."

Altgeld reserved his special wrath for the relationship between wealth and treatment under the law. Youthful first offenders who could not pay fines were quickly dispatched to prison, while "the crafty criminal—especially if he be rich—is gently dealt with." Altgeld demanded the end of different treatment for rich and poor. He insisted that the system of imposing fines be done away with; likewise, the system of paying police officers fees for the number of arrests and convictions accumulated must go. All cases should be brought to trial rapidly, so that the problem of bail would be minimized. In Altgeld's eyes, every effort should be bent to the goal of equal justice under law for all.

The new book would have been a significant public service had it done no more than expose evils of inequality in the courts and penal machinery. But Altgeld went even further, and called for a change in the spirit underlying the whole concept of judicial punishment. Rehabilitation is the only justification of the penal system, Altgeld argued, and everything in the penal system not contributing to the rehabilitation of the inmates therein should be abolished. To this end, he proposed two immediate and far-reaching reforms: The use of indeterminate sentences, by which convicts would be imprisoned and released according to their individual progress toward reformation; and a system of honorable, paid labor in prison, by which even a penniless convict could build up a nest-egg which he could use to establish himself after release from prison.

Altgeld's proposals received scant response from those in control of government, but the book was a valuable tool in the hands of reformers. It won Altgeld the admiration of many of the leading thinkers and humanitarians of the day, and it brought him his two most able and devoted lieutenants—labor leader George A. Schilling and lawyer Clarence Darrow. In fact, the book had a great deal to do with starting Darrow on his own road to fame; after reading it, Darrow introduced himself to Altgeld, who in turn helped bring Darrow from Ohio and establish him in a Chicago law practice. They became law partners, and their mutual scorn for the pompous and the artificial bound them together as comrades in social protest and social dissent.

Meantime, Altgeld was preparing himself to once again enter the political arena. In 1884 he ran for Congress. Even though he was a Democrat running in a Republican district in a Republican year, he won some forty-five per cent of the votes cast.

Indeed, it had been a coalition that had first carried Altgeld to political victory years before in Missouri, when he was both Democratic and Granger nominee; and two years after his Illinois Congressional bid, another coalition had formed behind him. In 1886, as the nominee of the Democratic Party and the United Labor Party, Altgeld was elected a judge of the Cook County superior court. The onetime prosecutor, now a reformer, had won the approval of the people of Chicago to dispense justice for them.

In addition to Judge Altgeld, the United Labor Party won election of other candidates, including eight members of the state legislature. Labor dissatisfaction was at a high; workers had been agitating for an eight-hour day, and the police had reacted with violence. Peaceful labor meetings were broken up and unarmed laborers were brutally assaulted by policemen. Several Chicago workers had been killed in such incidents, and on the night of May 4, 1886, six months before Altgeld's election, a mass rally to protest police brutality was scheduled at Chicago's Haymarket.

Several thousand persons assembled to hear addresses by Chicago labor leaders. The meeting was peaceful and orderly. Mayor Carter Harrison attended and had no fear in mingling with the crowd. Terming the meeting harmless, the Mayor told police officials not to trouble themselves further by standing by; he advised they follow his own example and go home. Meantime, the meeting itself had almost concluded; the crowd had dwindled, and only a thousand or so remained as the last speakers were summing up.

But as soon as the Mayor left, Captain John Bonfield drew up a formation of almost two hundred policemen and prepared to attack the meeting. From somewhere, a bomb was thrown and a number of policemen went down, many injured and several dying. The police then opened fire on the unarmed workers and their families.

It was impossible to learn who had thrown the bomb. Even so, eight Chicago labor leaders—August Spies, Albert Parsons, Louis Lingg, Michael Schwab, Samuel Fielden, George Engle, Adolph Fischer, and Oscar Neebe—were put on trial. The prosecution acknowledged that none of them was directly involved with the throwing of the bomb, or even knew that a bomb was to be thrown. But it was charged that each and all of them had been advocating labor reform, to be accomplished at the cost of violence if necessary, and, therefore, they had brought about the atmosphere which had incited the bombing. They were tried in Chicago before Judge Joseph E. Gary. All were found guilty, and on October 7, 1886, they were sentenced—fifteen years in the penetentiary for Neebe, and death by hanging for the remaining seven.

This trial of the so-called "Haymarket Anarchists" received international attention. Members of the Altgeld circle, particularly Schilling and Darrow, were in the forefront of those who condemned the trial. Business leaders and newspapers whipped up hysteria throughout the trial and afterward, playing on prejudice against socialists, anarchists, and immigrants. But there was a great undercurrent of sympathy among the workers, indicated by the fact that only a month after Judge Gary had imposed sentence on the Haymarket leaders, the voters placed Altgeld beside him on the Cook County superior court. Not only did Altgeld and Gary present a vivid contrast as jurists and men, but a personal antagonism was to accentuate their clashes on the bench and later in life.

How different might have been the judicial treatment of the Haymarket leaders had they been tried before Altgeld; but he arrived on the bench too late. Judicial appeals to higher courts failed. Fielden and Schwab finally received executive clemency from Governor Oglesby, who commuted their sentences to life imprisonment. Lingg escaped the hangman by committing suicide in his cell. On November 11, 1887—barely a year after Altgeld became a judge—Spies, Parsons, Engle, and Fischer were hanged. Altgeld could do nothing, but he remembered—and waited.

As a judge, Altgeld strived for impartiality. Although his personal views strongly favored the cause of labor, he allowed himself to be guided according to the merits of each case brought before him. His judicious conduct won the respect of all quarters, and in 1890 Altgeld's colleagues on the bench elected him chief judge of the Cook County superior court.

Meantime, Altgeld continued and extended his business activities. His real estate ventures reached as far as Ohio. One successful transaction followed another, and Altgeld the reformer and jurist found himself a millionaire. His political influence was growing all the while. As a judge he could not and would not take an open and active role in politics, but this did not prevent him from planning political maneuvers which toppled Chicago's Republican organization and replaced the incumbent Republican mayor with a Democrat. Altgeld utilized the occasion to install Darrow as Chicago corporation counsel.

The appearance several years before of his book on penal reform had been greeted as a public service, and now he published a second volume, *Live Questions*. This new book ranged over a wide variety of topics, giving Altgeld's views on law and jurisprudence, on contemporary politics and politicians, and on economic and social questions. On all these subjects, Altgeld espoused a liberal Jeffersonianism and offered many specific goals for reform.

He was now carrying forward four careers—judge, businessman, author, and political leader. He was also preparing to launch the major building project of his career, an imposing new office building which was intended to dominate the heart of Chicago. He had been quoted as saying, "I have no children; I have to create something, and so I am creating buildings." On one of the most expensive plots of land in the city, Altgeld's vision began to take form; a sixteen-story office structure he proudly named the Unity Building.

The pressure of his various careers and the effect of little time and little rest on his responsibilities as a judge worried

Altgeld. Consequently, in 1891, after five years of service on the bench, he resigned from the Cook County superior court. Nevertheless, his influence in law continued because, once no longer a judge, he was freed from the limitations of the bench and could resume his full law practice.

The year 1891 was a pivotal one in Illinois politics. For one thing, a long-overdue reform had finally won out; the Australian ballot was adopted. Electoral frauds were no longer as simple as before, and professional politicians of both parties were compelled to take a long, hard look at prospective nominees. Now, more than ever, it was important for party leaders to get dynamic candidates who could attract a large following on their own.

And times were changing rapidly. Populist feeling was running strong. The Democratic party, long out of power, saw an opportunity to regain its old position of prominence. Farmers were angry at the railroads and the trusts; industrial workers chafed under the power of the big corporations; liberals and reformers were indignant at social conditions; immigrants and the children of immigrants yearned to be accepted and take their rightful place as Americans, without discrimination. Democratic politicians searched for a leader who could bring together these groups and unite them under the Democratic banner.

Not only did John P. Altgeld have the background and following to attract all the key groups the Democratic party leaders considered essential for victory; he had the added advantage of being a millionaire who was able and prepared to finance his own campaign. Altgeld was selected to head the 1892 Democratic state ticket as gubernatorial nominee. Declining contributions, he paid out $100,000 to cover all his campaign expenses in full. And he won, becoming the first Democratic governor of Illinois in decades, the first foreign-born governor ever, and the first governor who was a Chicagoan.

But for Altgeld, the battle did not end with the election. He had spent more than a small fortune from his own resources; he had spent his health. Many thought that Altgeld would not be able to take charge of the office he had won at so dear a cost. But he was on hand to take the oath of office, and on January 10, 1893, he stood before the state legislature and delivered his inaugural address.

In his first address as chief executive, Altgeld presented a series of attacks on contemporary conditions. He condemned the conditions and treatment under which workmen were compelled to toil and live, and he particularly attacked child labor; he condemned the conditions in the state hospital and prisons; and he condemned the whole system of law enforcement as it discriminated against the poor. He pledged himself and his administration to eradicate all these evils insofar as the state government had power to do so. Those who had dismissed Altgeld's expressed views as mere political talk were now surprised, even shocked, to learn that he intended to attempt to put those views into practice.

As Governor, Altgeld had obligations to the Democratic organization which had supported him. He made no pretense of being nonpartisan, but dispensed patronage freely, cheerfully displacing Republicans and replacing them with Democrats. However, he used a more discriminating standard in regard to administrative posts responsible for certain key social problems. George A. Schilling, a labor leader of integrity and an Altgeld lieutenant for many years, became the new Governor's adviser and administrator concerning labor affairs. Another Altgeld appointee was Florence Kelley, one of the dedicated women of Chicago's Hull House, who, as chief factory inspector for the state, achieved much in alleviating child labor and sweatshop conditions.

A few days after his inauguration, Governor Altgeld had sent for the records of the Haymarket case. But months then passed and he gave no indication of what he would do, if anything. Issue a pardon on the basis of mercy, many of his supporters and others urged. Governor Oglesby had made the first move in this direction when he had commuted the sentences of Fielden and Schwab from death to life imprisonment. Then, over the years, many prominent and eminently respectable people had urged a pardon on the ground of mercy. So, his advisers told Altgeld, cite Oglesby's action and the petitions for mercy as justification, then issue a limited pardon which would further reduce the sentences of Fielden and Schwab and would free

Neebe. Such a course would satisfy liberal and labor groups and would at the same time be politically safe.

Altgeld soon put aside consideration of such a course of action, and rebuffed those who continued to advocate it. In Altgeld's mind, the issue was simple: The defendants were either guilty or not guilty. If they were guilty, then their sentences were not too severe for murderers, and mercy was not warranted. If they were innocent, they should not have suffered any punishment at all.

If a limited pardon on the ground of mercy involved some political risk, then to consider an unconditional pardon on the ground that the convictions were obtained unjustly and illegally was to court complete political disaster—and none knew it better than Altgeld. When he was warned of the danger inherent in such a course, Altgeld was said to have retorted: "If I decide they were innocent I will pardon them, by God, no matter what happens to my career."

Unknown to all but a few, Altgeld already was gathering the final details of evidence needed to sustain a pardon which would openly claim to reverse a miscarriage of justice. On June 26, 1893, he issued a pardon 18,000 words long, a document which was devastating in its thoroughness.

Another crisis of state leadership was approaching. As months passed, labor unrest in Illinois intensified. In his Labor Day address of 1893, "Address to the Laboring Men of Chicago," Altgeld predicted even bleaker days ahead. The deepening depression justified his worst fears. The state administration under Altgeld did everything possible to help the unemployed and destitute. And, when need be, Altgeld attempted to avert industrial violence by sending the militia to enforce an impartial peace. But these measures were but small assistance in terms of the general picture. Worker, farmer, and small businessman suffered alike. Only the giant corporations, with huge financial reserves, prospered. When lowered purchasing power reduced demands for goods and services, these corporations merely closed down part of their operations, thus laying off thousands of workers and sending them out to join the multitudes of unemployed already roaming the streets. The workers who were permitted to remain generally were forced to take wage cuts. But the corporations themselves remained as solvent and powerful as ever.

The despair was particularly keen in the company town of Pullman. Originally an independent section in the larger community of Hyde Park, it became a part of Chicago along with the entire Hyde Park area. The dwellers in George Pullman's town worked in the Pullman factories, lived in company-owned homes, purchased from company-approved stores, and in general were treated as the private property of George M. Pullman and his chief financial associate, Marshall Field.

As the depression grew worse, more Pullman workers joined those who already had suffered wage cuts, and still others were laid off. But, although Pullman wages fell, the rents and prices in Pullman's town remained at the same high rate. Those that complained were discharged altogether. Finally, in May of 1894, the Pullman workers went on strike. Within a month, the American Railway Union came to their support by refusing to operate trains carrying Pullman cars.

Without warning, the federal government suddenly moved into action. President Cleveland's Attorney General, Richard Olney, himself a former railroad attorney, arranged for a federal court injunction declaring the strike illegal. His next step was to have the federal marshal mobilize a small army of several thousand deputies, who, incidentally, were paid not by the government but by the railroads. Chicago, peaceful until then, saw conflict as soon as these deputies moved against the workers. This, in turn, gave Attorney General Olney the chance to send federal troops into Chicago.

Governor Altgeld had been standing by with regiments of Illinois troops in readiness, but he was ignored by Olney, who was charged by labor sympathizers as being more interested in breaking the strike than restoring order. The arrival of federal troops to join the federal deputies caused further violence. Finally, Mayor John P. Hopkins of Chicago appealed to Governor Altgeld for state troops, and the Illinois militia entered the city.

The state troops quickly restored order but the strike already was lost. Eugene Victor Debs and other labor leaders had been arrested by federal authorities and were speedly committed to federal prison. Altgeld vainly protested the federal actions and, as a result, was strongly denounced throughout the nation.

For the time being, President Cleveland had bested Governor Altgeld. But Cleveland's treatment of Illinois workers and the manner in which he had bypassed the state government left Altgeld with an unrelenting bitterness toward the President and his administration. There had always been a wide ideological gulf between these two Democratic leaders; now Cleveland added personal antagonism to the relationship.

Rumblings of discontent against the national Democratic leadership intensified within the party during 1894-96. Democrats already were divided on various issues, and now the growing struggle between the free silver and gold standard forces widened the split. The Populist spirit was on the march. William Jennings Bryan, the "Boy Orator of the Platte," was electrifying audiences throughout the West and further arousing them against the Cleveland group. The passage of time and the drift of events both had favored Altgeld, and now he found great sympathy for his ideas among Democratic politicians as well as the rank-and-file. The final step was the selection of Chicago—Altgeld's home ground—as the site of the 1896 Democratic National Convention.

The convention, held in July, was a disaster for President Cleveland and his followers. On every issue, Altgeld's views prevailed. Altgeld probably could have had the Presidential nomination for the asking, had he not been disqualified by place of birth. As it was, he secured the nomination for Bryan and dictated the platform on which Bryan was to run.

But the triumph of July faded into the defeat of November, as the full force of Mark Hanna's Republican machine rolled over the Democrats. Even so, Bryan made a surprisingly good showing. In a period of but a few months, he and Altgeld had taken control of a national party, ousted its old leadership, reformed the party ideologically, and gone before the voters with a startlingly new platform which has since been described as the most radical ever adopted by a major political party in the United States. The Cleveland faction and many of the Democrats who favored the gold standard defected, and actively harassed the national party. And the Democratic ticket was faced with canny Republican opposition. Altgeld was to lament that the Democrats were "confronted by everything money could buy, that boodle could debauch, or that fear of starvation could coerce."

Despite handicaps, the Democrats did well. Bryan carried twenty-two of the forty-five states, and amassed forty-seven percent of the votes cast across the nation. But it was a defeat, nonetheless; not only did the national ticket go down, but Governor Altgeld was defeated in his own bid for re-election. Altgeld's opponents gladly took the opportunity to make his defeat as unpleasant as possible. Not only did Altgeld's detractors everywhere gloat, but his successor refused even to permit him to deliver the traditional farewell address made by every retiring governor.

Altgeld had entered politics as a vigorous man and an influential millionaire. He was spent in both health and fortune when he left the gubernatorial office. He returned to Chicago and rejoined Clarence Darrow in their old law practice, but continued to be an influential national figure. In 1900 he journeyed to Kansas City and helped to make the 1900 Democratic National Convention a repetition of the one four years before. The 1896 platform was largely reaffirmed, and Bryan was renominated. That fall, Altgeld again campaigned throughout the nation for Bryan in the latter's second unsuccessful try for the Presidency.

Twice Altgeld's ideas had been offered to the nation, and twice they were rejected. Still, he would not give them up. He busied himself with legal work, with speaking and civic activities, and with the completion of two new books. On March 11, 1902, after a long day in court as defense counsel followed by a speaking engagement in Joliet, Altgeld collapsed just as he concluded his address. He had suffered a cerebral hemorrhage. The next day, John Peter Altgeld was dead.

HENRY M. CHRISTMAN

THE EAGLE THAT IS FORGOTTEN

Sleep softly . . . eagle forgotten . . . under the stone
Time has its way with you there, and the clay has its own.

"We have buried him now," thought your foes, and in secret rejoiced.
They made a brave show of their mourning, their hatred unvoiced.
They had snarled at you, barked at you, foamed at you day after day;
Now you were ended. They praised you . . . and laid you away.

The others that mourned you in silence and terror and truth,
The widow bereft of her crust, and the boy without youth,
The mocked and the scorned and the wounded, the lame and the poor,
That should have remembered forever . . . remember no more.

Where are those lovers of yours, on what name do they call—
The lost, that in armies wept over your funeral pall?
They call on the names of a hundred high-valiant ones;
A hundred white eagles have risen, the sons of your sons.
The zeal in their wings is a zeal that your dreaming began,
The valor that wore out your soul in the service of man.

Sleep softly . . . eagle forgotten . . . under the stone.
Time has its way with you there and the clay has its own.
Sleep on, O brave-hearted, O wise man, that kindled the flame—
To live in mankind is far more than to live in a name;
To live in mankind, far, far more . . . than to live in a name.

Vachel Lindsay (1879-1931)

"THE ADMINISTRATION OF JUSTICE IN CHICAGO"

An open letter of February 12, 1889

Early in 1889, after he had been a judge of the Cook County superior court for more than two years and felt that he knew the shortcomings of the courts, Altgeld published this letter in the Chicago newspapers. Although it referred to reform measures then being considered by the state legislature, it went beyond the legislation at hand to present a graphic, authoritative description of the Chicago court system.

HON. SHERWOOD DIXON, House of Representatives, Springfield.

Dear Sir: In answer to your letter asking my views upon your bill, which provides that the judges of the trial courts may, under certain conditions, given an oral charge to a jury, permit me to say that I am not satisfied with your bill, because it does not go far enough; still, it is a step in the right direction, and I hope the General Assembly will take up the matter of regulating the practice in our courts, and treat it with that thoroughness which its importance demands.

The main objections to our system of practice in the common law courts, referring particularly to Cook County, are:

First. The uncertainty as to result without regard to the justice of a cause brought about in part by legislation, which experience has shown to have been unwise, in part by requiring a unanimous verdict, and in part by the fact that the higher courts have embarrassed and complicated the administration of justice by what have been called "frivolous technicalities," applied not to the merits of a cause but to some question of procedure, so that hundreds of cases are reversed and kept hanging in the courts for years, until the subject-matter of litigation is lost and the parties are worn out with expense and worry—not because the case had been wrongly decided in the trial court upon the merits, but solely because there was a difference of opinion concerning some question of procedure. Consequently, dishonest men, with no meritorious defense, are encouraged to litigate, and, as a matter of fact, have almost as good a chance of success— at least for several years—as those that have an honest case, and many honest men with meritorious cases are afraid to go into the courts because they feel that they have only a little better chance there than a scoundrel.

Second. Another objection is that at present a lawsuit costs him who loses but little, if any more, than he who wins; so a man without a just cause of action or meritorious defense can keep a case in the courts for years and subject his opponent to great expense and annoyance without taking any chances. As a result, many suits are brought which ought not to be, and many others, in which there is no defense, are fought for years, simply because an unscrupulous defendant finds it to his advantage to fight rather than to settle. So that many meritorious cases are kept out of the courts, while our dockets are crowded with cases many of which ought not to be there, and many others of which should be speedily disposed of.

Third. Another objection is unreasonable delay. This grows out of the conditions I have just mentioned, and at the same time augments them. As a rule, it now takes from two to four years to dispose of a suit in our common law courts, whereas it should not take over forty days. At present, when a man begins a suit, he generally has to wait nearly two years before it comes up; in the meantime, the situation of the parties may have changed, or the subject-matter of the suit become worthless. Then he is notified by his lawyer that his case is about to be reached and that he must prepare for trial. Thereupon he partially neglects his business, has consultations with his lawyer, and looks around for his witnesses. In the course of a few days— or a few weeks—the case is actually placed on the call for the following day. Then he attends court with his witnesses for from two to ten days at great expense until the case is reached on the call, when it is discovered that on account of the engagement of counsel on one side or the other in some other court the case has to be passed for a short time. Then in the course of a week— or sometimes of three or four weeks—he gets his witnesses together again and goes to the court-house, where he finds some other case on trial, and he is told to wait. In the course of a day or two his case is again reached, when the chances are about two to one that it will again have to be passed. And very frequently, after having neglected his business for weeks, and having been to great expense and trouble in getting his witnesses and attending court, it is found that on account of absent witnesses or some other cause the case must be continued, and that it will not be reached again for upward of a year, when he will have all his work and trouble of preparation, etc., to do over again. If, however, the trial is begun, then he is astonished to find that it is apparently not the justice of his cause which is the main subject of inquiry, but that, instead, it is the rules of procedure about which great solicitude is shown. When the evidence is all heard and the lawyers have made their arguments, then he learns that we have had legislation in this State which changed the practice as it existed at common law and still prevails in the Federal courts, by which the judge was to point out to the jury just what the issues are, and state to them the law governing the case; but that, instead, the judge cannot give the jury any other than written instructions. As a consequence the jury is often left with very confused notions as to what the issues of fact are; and as there is usually not time for a judge to write out a clear and concise charge covering the whole case after the evidence is closed, he is frequently obliged to give a number of instructions prepared by counsel for the respective parties, and which frequently fail to give to the jury much light or guidance; so that the jury is liable to either bring in a verdict which is entirely wrong and must be set aside, or else to disagree and thus compel the parties to wait until the case is again reached in its order, and then do all this work over again. As the law requires a unanimous verdict, the suitor finds that if there should be a corrupt man on the panel, or a crank, or a man who felt

offended at something said by another juror, he has it in his
power to produce a miscarriage of justice without giving any
reason. If, however, the suitor safely runs all these gauntlets
and secures a verdict, which after a motion for a new trial has
been argued, is left to stand, then a judgment is entered, and
the defendant appeals to the appellate court. This takes about
one year more, and occasions considerable expense for lawyers'
fees, printing, etc. Then it is found that the appellate court
reverses about forty per cent of all cases brought to it, and sends
them back to be tried over again; and they are reversed, as a
rule, not on the merits—not because an actual injustice has
been done, but a great majority of cases are reversed because
of what has been styled "some frivolous error" in the procedure.
Frequently some point which neither side thought of or urged
in the court below is made a ground for reversal, because, to
quote the language of the higher courts, "it may have influenced
the jury"; not that it probably did influence the jury, or that the
result should have been different on the evidence. So that our
suitor finds that two chances out of five are against him in the
higher court. If his case is reversed and sent back, then he finds
himself just where he was when he started, and he has had upward of three years of expense, trouble, and worry for nothing.
He must do all his work over again, and it will require from
two to four more years to get through with it. If, on the other
hand, his case is affirmed by the appellate court, then, if the
amount involved exceeds one thousand dollars, an appeal is again
taken to the supreme court. This involves another delay of about
a year, and the paying of lawyer's fees, printers' fees, etc. Here
again his case may be reversed and sent back, and if it is, the
suitor finds himself just where he started, and all his outlays and
his worry has been for nothing. But as the supreme court at
present cannot review the facts, but considers only questions of
law, the chances of a reversal here are not so great. If the judgment is affirmed so that the lawsuit is finally ended, then he
learns that the other—that is, the losing—side need pay him
nothing for all the expense, delay, and trouble to which he had
been subjected, even though his suit was founded on a promissory
note. That is, a man with ever so honest a claim may be kept
in the courts for years, kept out of the use of his money and

put to great expense and trouble, and the other side need not pay his lawyers' fees, need not pay the printer's bills, need not pay for the delay, nor for the trouble and annoyance to which he has been subjected.

Is it any wonder that many of our business men would rather lose a claim entirely than to go into court with it? Is it any wonder that many conscientious lawyers advise their clients to accept any kind of a settlement rather than attempt to litigate? Is it not reasonably certain that if the law were to provide that every time a case is decided on its merits in any court of record the court shall fix a reasonable attorney-fee to be paid by the losing party to the winning party, it would weed out much of the litigation we now have, and bring about a condition in which a man having an honest claim would not feel that he might as well lose it all as to go into a court of justice with it?

Fourth. Still another objection urged with much force is that our present system entails a heavy expense on the public—on the non-litigating people—which they ought not to pay.

Leaving out of consideration the probate and the county courts, which to a certain extent are administrative, there are in Cook county eighteen judges, including the superior and the circuit court judges. Two of these are constantly at the criminal court, leaving sixteen attending to civil business. It is true three of these are in the appellate court, but their salaries have to be charged to the public.

The salaries of these sixteen amount to.................. $112,000
The expense of the clerks' offices of the superior and circuit
    courts for a year is...............................   69,468
The expense of sheriff's office, chargeable to these two
    courts, over and above its earnings, is.................   75,000
The expense of keeping up court-house, and chargeable to
    these two courts, is..............................   20,000
The jurors' fees for these two courts amount to...........   62,756
                                            ————
      Total....................................... $339,124
The total earnings of the superior and of the circuit court
    clerks' offices amount to.......................... 107,487
                                            ————
                                         $231,737

Leaving $231,737 as the sum which the people of Cook County pay annually for the benefit of its litigants. The present fee to be paid on commencing a suit is $6; and by a defendant on entering an appearance is $1.50.

The total number of suits brought, including appeals from justices, in the superior and the circuit courts during the year 1888, was 12,380, as follows: 3,460 suits in chancery; 7,960 suits at law; and 2,325 appeals from justices.

They were disposed of as follows: Judgment entered by default or confessions, 2,759; 3,039 were dismissed for want of prosecution, and 3,407 were tried. So that there were about 3,000 more cases brought during the year than were disposed of.

If we take $339,224, the total expense to the public, and divide it by 12,380, the total number of suits brought, we have $27.40, the amount which each suit should contribute in order to defray the expense; or if we divide by 9,205, the number of cases disposed of, we have $38.59 which each case should contribute.

But as it would be unjust to require a small case, which consumes but a few hours, to contribute as much as one taking up several days, it would perhaps be better to repeal the statute which provides that in Cook County $6 advanced by the plaintiff and $1.50 by the defendant shall be in full of all costs to be paid to the clerk of the court. In that case the clerk would collect fees for everything that is done and turn them over to the county treasurer, as is now the practice throughout the State; and it is believed that this would give ample funds to cover the whole expense. It may be added that the law limiting the fees to be paid in Cook County was passed at a time when the clerks pocketed all the fees paid and amassed vast fortunes. It was intended to limit their income. But since clerks are paid a salary and are required to pay all fees into the county treasury, the reason for the law has ceased to exist. If, however, the statute cannot be repealed, then I would leave the fees as they are, and suggest that the clerk be required to tax a fee of twenty-five dollars per day to be paid to the county for each day or fraction of a day consumed at the trial—this to be paid by the losing side, unless otherwise ordered by the court.

Referring again to the expense of keeping up our system of jurisprudence in proportion to results attained, I will add that the total amount of moneyed judgments rendered in the circuit

and superior courts of Cook County during the year 1888 was
$7,831,174, the greater part of which was in cases in which there
was default or a confession, and a very large per cent of which is
worthless because of the insolvency of the defendants. To this
work must be added judgments in cases seeking other than
moneyed relief, such as ejectment suits, injunction suits, etc.,
and suits in which it was sought to recover money but in which
the court found for defendant.

If we thus take the expense to the public, as already shown,
and add to this the expense to the litigants in the 12,380 cases,
in the way of lawyers' fees on both sides, witnesses' fees or time
on both sides, incidental expenses on both sides, loss of time
and neglect of business on both sides in preparing for trial, attending court, etc., to say nothing of the worry and anxiety—
it is a question whether the cost will not exceed the total results attained—that is, whether it does not on the average cost
us more to secure for a man his rights than they are worth to
him. Just what this expense and loss to litigants and witnesses
would average, it is of course impossible to say. It has been
variously estimated at from $150 to $250 to each side, or from
$300 to $500 in each case. If this estimate is nearly correct, then
there is little doubt that the expense and loss amount to more
than can be realized on all the judgments rendered, or than
would have been required to settle all matters in dispute.

There can be no doubt that, if we had encouraged arbitration,
instead of discouraging it, a great saving would have been ef-
fected to both public and litigants. But instead of encouraging
a speedy adjustment of disputes, by having parties submit their
claims to arbitrators selected by themselves, the courts have
almost invited the party defeated in an arbitration to come into
court and tie the whole matter up for several years, and then
have often set the award aside on purely technical grounds.

What I would respectfully urge upon the consideration of
the General Assembly is an amendment of the law so as to provide:

First. That in all courts of record in this State the judge shall
orally state the law governing the case, as was the practice at
common law and is now the practice in the Federal courts.

Upon this point I will simply add that the statute requiring the instructions to be in writing was passed in order that there should be no dispute as to what the charge was; and inasmuch as the law at present provides for a stenographer to attend the sittings of every circuit court to report the proceedings, the reason for requiring that the instructions be in writing no longer exists; and as there generally is not time to write a comprehensive charge, and, consequently, cases are frequently submitted in an unsatisfactory manner to a jury, the law should be changed. What we need is to restore trial by jury more nearly to the condition and form in which it existed at the common law and still exists in the Federal courts, taking away, however, the power of one man to thwart justice; and when this is done, this system of trial will remain the best that has yet been devised. On the last point I will add that, in all other important, and even vital matters, we accept the decision of the majority. A majority settles all questions of taxation and expenditure, all questions of peace and of war. A majority decides who shall make the laws. A majority decides what shall be law, and, finally, a majority decides who shall interpret and administer the law. In short, questions which reach to the very hearthstone of the citizen, and involve the existence of our institutions, are settled by the majority, and if, concerning any of these matters, a man were to urge absolute unanimity, we would question his sanity. But in determining a dispute over property, we put it into the power of one man—be he rogue, or crank, or sullen fool—without any risk to make a miscarriage of justice, or a farce out of a proceeding which may have consumed days and have cost both the public and the litigants large sums of money. And when asked why we permit such an anomaly, our only answer is, that they did things in this way more than a hundred years ago; when in truth trial by jury then was a very different thing from what it is to-day, for then the judge practically tried the case. If in civil cases we were now to accept a verdict of three-fourths of a panel, we would preserve all that is conservative and useful in our jury system, and would put an end to the "funny verdicts" that we hear about, and which are generally due to one man; and particularly we would put an end to the tampering with justice, which in large cities is a serious evil. I am in favor of trial by jury, and am opposed to its abolition; but the system is now so

THE ADMINISTRATION OF JUSTICE IN CHICAGO   23

hampered as to make it a kind of absurdity. Let us make it a rational institution, and it will command the respect of everybody.

Second. That when rendering judgment on the merits in any case in a court of record, the court shall fix a reasonable attorney-fee, to be paid by the losing party to the winning party: Provided, that if it appears that an offer to compromise had been made and kept good by the losing party, and no more is recovered than had been offered, then no attorney-fee shall be allowed for what was done thereafter; and provided, that an attorney-fee shall only be allowed for trying a case on the merits.

Third. Either let the clerk of the court collect fees for everything that is done, and turn them into the county treasury, or else tax as costs, to go to the county, a reasonable sum for every day, or fraction thereof, which a case consumes at the trial; so that the non-litigating public may at least partially be relieved of the burden of expense created solely by litigants.

Fourth. That before any appellate court or the supreme court shall reverse a case and send it back to be tried over, the judges of such court, or a majority thereof, shall state, in writing, that an injustice has been done the appellant in the judgment on the merits by the trial court; and shall also specify wherein such injustice consists.

As to this fourth suggestion, I will simply say that if the framers of the Constitution, and the people in adopting it, intended, in creating a system of jurisprudence, that courts should be places for lawyers to fence and judges to theorize, and that cases should be treated simply as a corpse in a dissecting-room—that is, used illustrate a principle—then no change should be made, for in many cases the present system produces everything that could then be desired. But if the object in creating and maintaining courts was to do justice between man and man, and if rules of procedure was to be used simply as means to this end, then no reasonable objection can be urged against this provision. The trouble now is that we lift cases into the domain of opinion where there always is a diversity of views, and then, on points which settle nothing and do not decide the merits, we keep cases bounding backward and forward like a foot-ball, to the ruin of litigants—the appellate court reversing the trial court, and the supreme court reversing the appellate court.

Fifth. That if a matter is submitted to arbitration, the award shall be final, and shall be set aside only for fraud; and that when set aside, the arbitrators shall make a new award; and that in cases of mistake, or where the award is uncertain, the arbitrators may amend it or correct it.

In conclusion, let me remark that in the mercantile world, in the manufacturing world, in agriculture, in medicine, in fact, in nearly every field of knowledge or human activity, there has been an advance, a steady improvement, a movement in the line of common sense, an honest effort to keep abreast of the spirit of the nineteenth century; while in our methods of administering justice we seem rather to have retrograded. What changes we have made in this State have tended rather to complicate than to simplify. A century ago trial by jury in civil causes was simple, expeditious, and, upon the whole, satisfactory. We have hampered and crippled it in its workings until many good people are seriously advocating its abolition. A century ago the courts of appeal wrote opinions that were short and to the point, and generally decisive of the case; now, courts of appeal, not only in this State, write long essays—learned disquisitions which frequently evade the main questions and settle nothing. On behalf of our great profession, I ask, "Cannot we, also, go forward?"

Very truly yours,
JOHN P. ALTGELD,
Judge of the Superior Court.

Chicago, February 12, 1889.

"THE IMMIGRANT'S ANSWER"

An article published in the February, 1890, issue of The Forum *magazine*

The many immigrants who flocked to America during Altgeld's day, and those Americans whose parents had come from Europe, looked to him as a natural leader. Born in Germany, a fluent speaker who addressed public gatherings in both English and German, a successful lawyer and businessman who nonetheless remembered his humble origin, he was a logical spokesman for their cause. This article presented his viewpoint in regard to immigration and naturalization.

The question whether immigration shall be encouraged or restricted, and whether naturalization shall be made more difficult or not, must be considered both from a political and from an industrial point of view; and in each case it is necessary to glance back and see what have been the character, the conduct, and the political leaning of the immigrant, and what he has done to develop and enrich our country. Has he been law-abiding, industrious, and patriotic, and is the government indebted to him for anything; or is it a case of a spoilt pauper child housed, fed, and clothed in a fine Christian uniform, all at the expense of native Americans, and to no purpose?

We will look at the political side first, and, as our space is limited, we will go back only to 1860, calling attention, however, to the fact that up to that time, no matter from what cause, the immigration had been almost entirely to the Northern and free States, and not to the slave States, as will be seen by the figures about to be given. These, when carefully examined in connection with election returns, will show that but for the assistance of the immigrant the election of Abraham Lincoln as president of the United States would have been an impossibility, and that had the cry, "America for the Americans," prevailed at an earlier period of our history, the nineteenth century would never have seen the great free republic we see, and the shadow of millions of slaves would to-day darken and curse the continent.

I will cite no doubtful authority, but will take as a basis the United States census of 1860. The total population of the States was 31,183,744, of whom 4,099,152 were foreign born, and of the latter only 216,730 were to be found in all the eleven States which seceded. The remaining States had a total population of 22,-313,997, of whom 3,882,422, or a little over one sixth, were actually foreign-born. To these we must add their children, who, though native-born, yet, as a rule, held the same views, were controlled by the same motives and influences, spoke the same language, and generally acted with their elders; who, in short, for all practical purposes, and especially for our purpose, must be treated as a part of the immigrant population. If we add two children for each foreign-born person, we find that fully one half of the population of the States that remained true to the Union consisted of the foreign-born and their children, and was made up chiefly of Germans, Scandinavians, and Irish.

The Scandinavians have always, nearly to a man, voted the Republican ticket. The Germans, likewise, were nearly all Republicans. In fact, the States having either a large Scandinavian or a large German population have been distinguished as the banner Republican States. Notably is this true of Iowa, Wisconsin, Minnesota, and Michigan, which have a large Scandinavian population; and of Illinois, Ohio, and Pennsylvania, which have a very large German population. The Irish more generally voted the Democratic ticket, but were not united; and in New York, where they were most numerous, they have repeatedly given the Republican ticket substantial aid. Taking the States in detail, Iowa had a total population of 674,913. Of these 106,077, or about one sixth, were foreign-born, and nearly all were Germans and Scandinavians, who, to a man voted the Republican ticket. The total vote cast for President in Iowa in

1860 was 128,331, of which Lincoln received 70,409, giving him a plurality over Douglas of 15,298. Now, if simply the actual foreign-born vote had been left out, it would have amounted to one sixth of the whole, or 21,388. These would nearly all have been taken from Lincoln's vote, which would thus be reduced to less than 50,000, leaving to Douglas a plurality of over 5,000; and if instead of subtracting only the foreign-born vote, we were to subtract the vote which for our purpose must be regarded as immigrant, Lincoln's vote would be reduced to less than 40,000.

Wisconsin had a total population of 775,881. Of these, 276,967, or a little over thirty-five per cent., were foreign-born, nearly all Germans and Scandinavians, and they supported the Republican ticket. The total vote of Wisconsin in that year was 152,180, of which Lincoln received 86,110, giving him a plurality over Douglas of 21,089. Now, if the foreign-born vote were omitted, the total vote would be reduced by about thirty-five per cent., or 52,263; and nearly the whole of this would have to be deducted from Lincoln's vote, thus not only wiping out his plurality, but giving Douglas a plurality of nearly 30,000—this by deducting only the actual foreign-born vote, and not the additional vote, which, as we have seen, should be included.

Michigan had in that year a total population of 749,113. Of these, 149,093, or about one fifth, were foreign-born, nearly all Scandinavians, Hollanders, and Germans, and almost solidly Republican. The total vote of Michigan was 154,747, of which Lincoln received 88,480, giving him a plurality over Douglas of 23,423. If the foreign-born vote, amounting to about one-fifth, or 31,000, be left out, nearly all the loss must fall upon Lincoln's vote, giving Douglas a plurality.

Illinois had a population of 1,711,951, of whom 324,643, or almost one-fifth, were foreign-born. Of these, 87,573 were Irish, the remainder nearly all Germans and Scandinavians, adherents of the Republican party. Of the total vote of Illinois, 338,693, Lincoln received 172,161, giving him a plurality over Douglas of 11,946. If the actual foreign-born vote is to be eliminated, that reduces the total nearly one fifth, or upward of 66,000. Supposing the Irish foreign-born vote to have been solidly Democratic, which it was not, about 40,000 would still have to be deducted from Lincoln's vote; this would not only wipe out his plurality, but would give a very large plurality to Douglas.

Ohio's population was 2,339,500. Of these, 328,249, or about one seventh, were foreign-born, 76,826 being Irish, and the remainder mostly Germans, who, as a rule, were Republicans. The total vote of Ohio was 442,441, of which Lincoln received 221,-610—a plurality over Douglas of 34,378. If the foreign-born vote had been omitted, the total would have been reduced by nearly one seventh, or about 63,200. Assuming that most of the Irish were Democrats and voted for Douglas, nearly 50,000 votes would still have to be deducted from Lincoln's total, which would give the State to Douglas.

These five States alone are sufficient to demonstrate the situation; for if Lincoln had lost them and carried the other States in the Republican column, he would have had only 129 electoral votes, while he needed 151. But the facts are that in every State carried by Lincoln there was a large foreign population, which was mostly, and in some States entirely, Republican, and which continued to be Republican down to a very recent date; and if the vote of this class had been omitted in 1860, it would have reduced Lincoln's vote to such an extent as to defeat him in most of the States that he carried. I am speaking only of the foreign-born voters: but, as already shown, to these should be added a large percentage of the people who, although native-born, are of foreign-born parentage, and must be considered with them in viewing the general political course of immigrants. It is an indisputable fact that the vote of the naturalized citizen and of his son has been a most powerful and indispensable factor in giving the Republican party the control of the government; and even to-day its power and popularity are greatest in those States in which there is a large naturalized vote.

The eleven States that in 1861 hoisted the flag of secession had a population of 8,726,644. Of these, only 216,730, or about two and a half per cent., were foreign-born, and they were subsequently found to be Unionists. The men who sought to destroy our institutions, who proclaimed the principle of inequality, who insisted that the strong have a divine right to the fruit of the poor man's labor, and who finally fired upon the flag of the Republic, were not only Americans, but they were sons of Americans; while, on the other hand, the heavy German population of northern Kentucky and of Missouri, by their adherence to the Union, turned the scale and prevented two great States from giving their powerful aid to the Confederacy. The great majority of those that were Americans and sons of Americans in these two States were in favor of secession. Then, when the war began, those Northern States that had the largest foreign-born population furnished the largest quota of soldiers to the Union armies. Even Missouri contributed nearly 200,000 men, although it was the scene of repeated raids, during which a portion of its population, called by the Southern leaders "damned Dutch Unionists," was made to pay dearly for its patriotism. The records of the War Department show that of the 2,678,967 men that from first to last were enlisted in the Union armies, 494,900 were entered on the records as of foreign nationality. No doubt some of these were native born, but not very many, for, as a rule, the native-born recruits spoke the English languge and were booked as Americans. How many of these there were we cannot tell exactly, but, considering the fact that nearly half the population was of foreign nationality, and that recruits generally came from the common people, there is no question but that one half of the men who enlisted in the Union armies were either foreign-born or of foreign-born parentage. These would not have been here to enter our armies but for immigration, and better soldiers never marched to the music of war. There is not a swamp or field or dark ravine where treason made a stand, but is covered with the graves of Germans and Scandinavians who died for the principle of equal rights. Though the Irish more generally voted the Democratic ticket yet their patriotism was prompt to respond to the call of their adopted country, and there is not a battlefield where blood was shed for the Union that has not the bones of Irishmen rotting upon it.

Again, material resources are as necessary for the prosecution of a great war as are men, for the latter can do nothing without equipment, food, arms, and munitions of war. When the Rebellion collapsed, the South had yet large armies of men, but its resources were exhausted. It had no shoes, no food, no arms for its soldiers. It had not, within all its boundaries, sufficient ammunition to fight a great battle. The North, on the contrary, had yet inexhaustible resources, for it was largely indebted to the sober, steady, intelligent industry and frugality of its immigrant population; for those States in which this population was the largest were found to possess the best agriculture, the finest cities, the most shops, the largest factories, and the fullest warehouses. Further, the labor of building the great railway systems of our land, which are so necessary for the development of a country, and for the rapid concentration of men and material in time of war, was almost entirely done by these people.

Now, if Kentucky and Missouri had joined the Confederacy, and if the Northern States had not possessed the incalculable strength in both men and material resources that they got through the naturalized citizen and his children, they would not only have been unable to subdue the South, but they would have been unable successfully to resist Southern aggression: and some Southern colonel would to-day be calling the roll of his slaves in the shadow of Bunker Hill monument, for the country could not permanently have remained part slave and part free.

I do not claim that the foreigner gave to the country new ideas, nor do I wish in any manner to belittle the great achievements of the native Americans of the North; I am simply directing attention to the fact that, standing alone, they could not have elected Lincoln, could not have successfully resisted Southern aggression, and could not have put down the Rebellion; and that it was the naturalized citizen and his children, who, by joining hands with them, turned the scale in favor of the ideas and the institutions of the North, and thus directly helped to shape the destiny of our country.

In this connection, I wish to call attention to the remarkable historical fact that the great political party of the country that held out a friendly hand to the immigrant, and that favored and secured liberal naturalization laws, so that the new-comer could, in a reasonable time, become a citizen and voter, has been all along opposed and repeatedly defeated by these very naturalized voters; while, on the other hand, the great political party— first Federal, then Whig, and lastly Republican—from whose ranks has always come the opposition to a liberal naturalization law to make the new-comer a voter, and from whose ranks to-day comes, with increasing frequency, the cry of "America for the Americans," is the very party which has all along received by far the greater portion of this naturalized vote, was enabled by the aid of this very vote to keep control of the government for over a quarter of a century, and to-day is in power by the aid of this vote.

The one political party can truthfully say to the great majority of the naturalized voters: "I did what I could to give you the franchise, and you have constantly used that franchise to defeat me," while the other political party might truthfully say to the same people: "From my ranks has come all the opposition to you, and it is from my ranks that to-day comes the demand for restrictive naturalization laws; and in return for this treatment you have stood faithfully by me, have kept me in power, and have given office and honors to some of the very men who opposed and slandered you." It is incomprehensible why opposition to making a voter of the immigrant should come from members of the Republican party.

If we look at the question in still another light, it will be found that in those States which have the largest naturalized vote, and in which this has been a potent factor, there are more churches, more libraries, more schools, better schools, and more general intelligence than are to be found in those States where the people are not only American-born, but are the children of American-born parents. As a rule, the poor among the immigrants are more frugal, are more industrious, and are more used to continuous hard work than are the poor among native Americans, and consequently they generally succeed in making a living, while the latter frequently fail.

It has been charged against the naturalized citizen that he has at different times engaged in riots and disturbed social order; but in most of these cases it will be found that as many American-born as foreign-born have participated, the fact being that nationality had nothing to do with the matter, but that the disturbance grew out of industrial or political excitement. But even if this were not so, it does not lie in the mouth of an American to make this charge, for the most disgraceful acts of riot and mob violence that stain our annals were committed, not by the foreign-born in their rags, but by Americans dressed in broadcloth; and that not in a Dutch or an Irish settlement, but in the streets of Boston. This mob, known in history as the broadcloth mob, was diabolical in its fury, and sought to tear William Lloyd Garrison to pieces, not over a question of starvation wages, not to avenge an act of injustice and oppression, but simply because he had dared to proclaim that no man can have a right of property in another human being. If there have been mobs and riots among the foreign-born in our country, they were nothing but impotent protests, by ignorant though honest people, against that rapacious greed which took the bread they toiled for away from their children's mouths, while the broadcloth American Boston mob shrieked for the life of the man who dared to advocate human freedom.

I have been speaking, be it noted, of the immigrant who came of his own accord to our shores, with the purpose of renouncing forever his foreign allegiance, and swearing fealty to the republic. I do not include assisted paupers, habitual criminals, or laborers, whether yellow or white, brought over under contract to supplant and drive out American workmen, both native-born and naturalized. Against these classes our gates should be closed.

Coming now to the question, Shall naturalization be made more difficult? I ask: Why should it be? Does the history of the past furnish any reason for such legislation? If yea, what is it? If nay, then why begin now? If these people are to live here they should be a part of us, and should be made to feel that they have an interest in public affairs. To have a large foreign population among us and to deprive it of the right of citizenship, with all its privileges, would be to create jealousies, discontent, and, in short, the conditions which, in time, must produce disturbances, and in a critical juncture might endanger our political existence. We have seen that but for the vote and the influence of the naturalized citizen Lincoln could not have been elected, and that the destiny of our country must have been different.

But suppose this were not so; if the laws had prohibited a foreigner who had made his home among us from becoming a citizen, and if the millions of foreigners in this country that had accumulated property and acquired local influence had found themselves compelled to obey the laws and to pay taxes to support our institutions, while they had no voice in making those laws, in levying the taxes, or in managing those institutions, would they not have been discontented and secretly hostile to the government which thus treated them; and is it at all probable that when that government was attacked, either they or their sons would have rushed to its defense?

The idea of limiting the franchise is not new. Wherever and whenever there have been men who thanked God that they were not like their fellows, it has been advocated, and whereever it has been tried it has been a failure. It is simply the dying echo of aristocracy, and is inimical to the spirit of our institutions. Van Buren earned the gratitude of all true Republicans by striking it out of the constitution of New York. There are yet a few States in which a vestige of it remains; but it will be found that these States march not in the van, but with the lumber wagons of civilization.

It is frequently said that the people who come here are, as a rule, ignorant, and know nothing about our institutions, and therefore should not be permitted to vote after a residence of only five years; that they cannot act intelligently, and will simply be tools for crafty politicians to use at the expense of good government. Now, if the premises were true, the conclusions might seem plausible; and were it a matter of speculation only, they would, perhaps, be accepted. But the premises are false. Besides, this is no longer a matter of argument. We have had a century's experience and this must decide the question. If the vote of these people has, in the main, been marked by ignorance and been cast against beneficial measures and good government, then the charge must be accepted as true; on the other hand, if their vote has, in the main, been on the side of right and justice and good government, then the charge must be treated as being not only groundless, but a slander. We have already seen that the great majority of these votes has steadfastly been cast for the men and the measures which, for a quarter of a century have shaped the destiny of this nation; surely no voice from the Republican party will declare that they were wrong. This being so, no Republican should be permitted to make the charge of ignorance against a class of voters who helped to support these men and these measures, and without whose support the success of the latter would have been impossible.

In this connection it should be borne in mind that the so-called scholar is not the most intelligent, the most reliable, or the safest guide in public affairs. The great Selden was not joking when he affirmed that "no man is wiser for his learning, and no fool is a perfect fool until he learns Latin;" and Wendell Phillips was in dead earnest when he said:

Book learning does not make five per cent., of that mass of common sense that runs the world, transacts its business, secures its progress, trebles its power over nature, work out in the long run a rough average justice, wears away the world's restraints, and lifts off its burdens. Two-thirds of the inventions that enable France to double the world's sunshine, and make old and New England the workshops of the world, did not come from colleges or from minds trained in the schools of science, but struggled up from the irrepressible instinct of untrained natural power. Her workshops, not her colleges, made England for a while the mistress of the world, and the hardest job her workmen had was to make Oxford willing he should work his wonders. . . . Liberty and civilization are only fragments of rights wrung from the strong hands of wealth and book learning; almost all the great truths relating to society were not the result of scholarly meditation, but have been first heard in the solemn protests of martyred patriotism and the loud cries of crushed and starving labor. When common sense and the common people had stereotyped a principle into a statute, then book men came to explain how it was discovered."

I will add only that years ago, when the book men both North and South were learnedly demonstrating that slavery was a divine institution, these common people from foreign shores simply said, "It is wrong for one man to get another man's labor for nothing," and then took sides, not with the powerful and wealthy, but with the party that was then the object of ridicule, because it dared say that slavery was wrong. The history of this country demonstrates that the common people are swayed by a patriotic instinct or impulse in favor of the right—something which cannot be said of the wealthy or of the book men.

I know that occasionally the local government of a large city is cited to prove the ignorance of the naturalized voter; but only a superficial observer will make this assertion. This question has been examined by some of the ablest men of America and Europe, and they all agree that the cause of bad government at times in cities is partisanship and the saloon. And the saloon owes its power to the fact that it is courted by the local leaders of both political parties; each political party is ready and eager to make any combination which will enable it to defeat its opponent.

When the rich and the educated divide themselves up almost equally between the two great parties, and one half vote the Democratic ticket and the other half vote the Republican ticket; if then the naturalized voters, or, if you please, the common people, come along, and part vote the Republican ticket, the remainder the Democratic ticket, it is both nonsensical and dishonest to say that the result, no matter what it is, is due to the ignorance of the voters. Such a charge could be truthfully made only if substantially all the well-informed and the property-holding classes were to range themselves on one side, and the ignorant people on the other, and the latter were to carry the day and run things badly. But so long as the rich and the educated partisan in the Republican party will resort to any means to carry an election, and will stand in line with all classes of voters on that side, while the Democratic partisan does the same thing on the other side, the result must be attributed to a party and not to a class. There never was a dishonest government in any city in this country that did not come into power by the assistance of a large class of voters who not only were intelligent, but who boasted of American ancestry. And it is safe to say that there never will be one; for partisan feeling seems to blind men who are otherwise intelligent, fair, and honest, so that four out of five of the prominent and intelligent men in each political party will rather see their party win with men who are dishonest and unfit than see the opposite party win with honest and competent men. And, strange as it may seem, the man who comes to the polls in his carriage is, as a rule, more narrow and more bigoted than the poor man who has to lose half a day's wages in order to vote.

There is an objection to further immigration that at first blush seems plausible, namely, that it increases the competition among the unskilled laborers, who already find it impossible to maintain their families in a manner becoming even the humblest American citizen. Ocean travel has become cheap, safe, and speedy, and many European countries are overpopulated. These people are aware that in from two to three weeks they can go from the place of their birth to almost any part of the United States. They have heard of this country and have an exaggerated idea of its advantages; and the question naturally suggests itself: If these people are permitted to come, will not that reduce the unskilled laborer to the condition of the European laborer; and, to avoid this, would it not be better to prevent any more people from landing upon our shores? To a man who sympathizes with the American unskilled laborer, whether native-born or naturalized, in his hopeless condition, this argument, I repeat, at first seems plausible; but aside from the impossibility of enforcing such an exclusive policy along our sea-coast and four thousand miles of border crossed everywhere by railroads, there are insurmountable objections to it. First, it is contrary to the spirit of the age, and to the law of human development and the highest civilization, which require the freest intercourse possible, not only between men, but between nations; and no people ever yet profited, in the long run, by pursuing a policy at variance with this law. Secondly, it could be but a temporary expedient of such doubtful character that any great nation must hesitate to adopt it. Thirdly, it would be so decidedly narrow and provincial that, aside from its effect upon ourselves, we cannot take such a position in the face of the world. The truth is that the labor question is becoming more urgent, and the condition of the laborer is improving as fast in Europe as in this country: and the laborer's only hope for the future lies in united action, not alone in one country, but throughout the civilized world. This united action will be brought about much more quickly by unity of interest, free intercourse, and friendly co-operation, than would be possible if we were to isolate ourselves. In fact, it is only by this intercourse that the laboring masses can be so educated as to enable them to stand together, and by united action secure justice for themselves and their children; while isolation would prevent the spread of intelligence, make united action impossible, and thus put any great achievement out of the question.

Besides, the American laborer does not suffer very much from competition with the immigrant who comes of his own volition. The latter, coming here to improve his condition and that of his family, soon joins his American brother, and asks wages which will at least enable him to do this. But the condition of the laborer has been made deplorable by the importation of ship-loads of men under contract. These do not come with the motives or with the ambition of the class we have been consider-ing; they have no thought of becoming citizens, but are practi-cally slaves, who will work for wages upon which the American laborer cannot exist. Agents for large corporations are con-stantly importing them. Steamship companies, to get the passage money paid by American employers, bring them over by the thousands so that many great centers of industry in the East have been filled with them, and the American laborer is being crowded out. Both the native-born and the naturalized laborer have been almost driven out of the great State of Pennsylvania by these importations. True, there is a law against such con-tracts, but it is a dead letter; so that we have in this country the strange spectacle of the government keeping up the price of a great many articles by shutting out foreign competition, and at the same time permitting the manufacturers of these articles to import the pauper laborers of Europe to produce them.

But this is not natural immigration; and whether the people thus brought be Chinese, Hungarian, Polish, or British paupers, they should be excluded; but natural immigration should not be interfered with. Free circulation of the blood is necessary to a healthy growth, whether of an individual or of a nation, and any restriction of the natural processes arrests development and en-feebles both body and mind. Thousands of years ago the cry, "China for the Chinese," prevailed and became a law in one of the richest quarters of the globe, among a people that had already a high civilization. From that time their faces have been turned backward, and they have simply been worshiping the shades of their father; and yet there are in this age and in this country men who would have us practice Chinese statesmanship.

JOHN P. ALTGELD.

"WHAT SHALL WE DO WITH OUR CRIMINALS?"

Address delivered before the Sunset Club, Chicago, March 27, 1890

It was the cause of penal reform which first brought John P. Altgeld into a life of public service. In 1884 he published *Our Penal Machinery and Its Victims*, in which he strongly condemned the prevailing penal system. As a judge of the Cook County superior court, Altgeld continued to advocate an enlightened system of detention and correction.

Altgeld wanted more than a system with humane treatment. He wanted a system which would put aside the idea of retribution and punishment, and would instead work toward the speedy rehabilitation of offenders.

No man can examine the great penal system of this country without being astounded at its magnitude, its cost, and its unsatisfactory results. There are in the United States upward of 2,200 county jails, several hundred lock-ups, or police stations, between fifty and sixty penitentiaries, with workshops, machinery, etc. The first cost of erection of all these buildings and shops has been estimated at upward of $500,000,000, which is dead capital—the interest, at five per cent., upon which sum alone, would annually amount to $25,000,000. To this must be added the sums annually appropriated out of the treasury to feed the prisoners, pay the officers, judicial and executive, and keep up and maintain all these institutions, which sums have been estimated at upward of $50,000,000, to say nothing of the costs paid by the accused; there are, in addition to the many thousands of policemen and detectives, about 70,000 constables in this country, and about as many magistrates. There are upwards of 2,200 sheriffs, and in the neighborhood of 12,000 deputy sheriffs. Then come the grand juries, petit juries, judges, and lawyers; next the keepers and their numerous assistants for all these prisons. On the whole, there are about a million of men partly or wholly supporting their families from this source, and as I am on the list, I may speak with freedom, and say that, as a rule, they are comfortable, are anxious to hold on, and ready to defend the system which gives them and their families bread.

A glance at this system almost suggests the question whether society has any other object to care for, or mission to accomplish, than simply to maintain this machinery. Looking at its workings, we find that there are in the neighborhood of 75,000 convicts in the various penitentiaries. As the average sentence is about two years and one-half, the whole number, on the average, is therefore renewed once every two years and one-half; so that there are in the neighborhood of three-quarters of a million of men living in our midst who have had a penitentiary experience. We next see that upward of five per cent. of the entire population is arrested by the police and other officials every year; so that there are about three million people arrested and "run in" every year. Assuming that one-third of them are what are called "repeaters"—that is, have been arrested before—it would still leave two millions who are for the first time each year broken into what may be called a prison experience; and yet, notwithstanding the vast army of men employed, the millions annually expended, the numerous arrests, the large number imprisoned, crime is said to be increasing, and our whole penal system is pronounced to be a failure, both in this country and in Europe, where they have similar systems.

And the question is asked by thoughtful men: "What shall be done? Society must be protected. If the present system is a failure, what shall we substitute?" It has been but a few years since the general public gave this question any consideration. Heretofore the only remedy ever suggested or thought of was the application of brute force. In all the past centuries, and in every country on the globe, methods of punishment for the prevention of crime have prevailed which were the embodiment of brutality and of fiendish cruelty. The prisoners were often transformed into either raving maniacs or wild beasts, while the keepers of prisons became fiends in human form; and in all times, and in every country on the globe, this system of human torture was a failure. Brutality never yet protected society or helped humanity. There was a time in England when men were hanged or burned for trivial offenses; but instead of deterring, the very shadow of the gallows seemed to produce a crop of fresh offenders, and the glow of human embers invited new victims to the stake.

One difficulty with our system is that it proceeds on the idea of expiation—that is, paying for having violated the law. In feudal times every violation of law was a source of revenue to the feudal lord, or to the king. The fine was paid to him, or whatever penalty was paid went to him, the more serious of offenses being followed by a confiscation of property. The imposition, then, of a fine was one of the means employed by the strong to plunder the weak. Now we have advanced until theoretically we declare that crime should not be a source of revenue, and that it is only for the protection of society that punishment can be inflicted; yet when we come to impose penalties, we proceed upon the theory that if the offender pays for or expiates the violation, then that ends all. He can go right on and violate the law a second time, and if he pays the penalty all is wiped out. Instead of inquiring into the history, the environment, and the character of the offender, and then applying a treatment which will in reality protect society, we simply fix a price upon each infraction; and we treat those who are not vicious, but have been unfortunate, and have been guilty of some slight offense, in almost the same manner that we treat the vicious who have been guilty of graver offenses; and we put both in a condition in which it is next to impossible for either to make an honest living when they have been once imprisoned.

I desire to consider the subject rather from a practical than from a theoretical standpoint. The first important question that arises when we are brought face to face with the workings of our system is, Where do all these people who are arrested come from? What is the environment which produces them? As we have not the time to inquire extensively into home conditions, or the training of the youth, we will start at once at the point where they are first brought to our view, and that is in the police court, and we will soon see where they come from.

The report of the superintendent of police of Chicago for the year 1888 shows that in that year the police officers of Chicago alone arrested and carried to the lock-up 50,432 people, 40,867 of whom were males, 9,565 of whom were females. The great majority of them were under thirty years of age; nearly 9,000 were under twenty years of age; a little over 30,000 of them were American-born; the others were made up various nationalities. The same report shows that 10,263 were common laborers; 18,336 had no occupation; 1,975 were housekeepers. Some of you may ask: "What were these people arrested for, and what was done with them?" Well, the same report shows that upward of 15,000, or nearly one-third, were discharged in the police court because it was not proven that they had violated any law or ordinance; and out of the whole number arrested, only 2,192 were held over on criminal charges. The rest were fined for a violation of some ordinance, generally on the charge of disorderly conduct. The police magistrate having no power to try a charge of crime or grave misdemeanor, it follows that every case of that nature had to be sent to the grand jury; and I repeat that, out of the whole 50,000 only a little over 2,000 were held over; and the records of the criminal court show that, of these, more than two-thirds fell to the ground because no offense could be proven.

Bearing in mind that those arrested were young, that they came from the poorer classes, from those who are already fighting an unequal fight in the struggle for existence, I ask you what effect do you suppose the act of arresting them upon the street, possibly clubbing them, then marching them to the lock-up, and shoving them into a cell—what effect did all this have upon the 15,000 who were not shown to have been guilty of any offense, who had violated neither law of God nor statutes of man? They were treated while under arrest as if guilty of highway robbery. Did this treatment strengthen them and make them better able to hold their heads up, or did it tend to break their self-respect, to weaken them? Did it not embitter them against society and a system which had done them this wrong? Will they not feel the humiliation and degradation as long as they live; and will that very treatment not mark the beginning in many cases of a downward criminal career?

But we will follow the subject a little further. You are aware that when a fine is imposed in the police court, if it is not paid the defendant is taken to the house of correction—that is, the bridewell, which for all practical purposes is a penitentiary. It has for many years been in charge of Mr. Charles E. Felton, who is one of the most experienced and most intelligent prison managers in the United States. In his report for that year he says: "In the year 1888 the number of prisoners was 10,717, the average daily number imprisoned was 764½; the average duration of imprisonment was but 26.1 days. Of the above who were received during the year all save ninety-six were convicted for petty offenses, the executions under which they were imprisoned showing their offense to have been chiefly disorderly conduct, or other violation of municipal or town or village ordinance, mere petty misdemeanors, punishable by fine only, the imprisonment being the result of the non-payment of the fine."

Reflect upon this a moment: 10,717 were imprisoned during the year, and out of this number only ninety-six were convicted of criminal offenses. The others, in the language of Mr. Felton, were guilty of mere petty misdemeanors, punishable by fine only, and they were imprisoned because they could not pay this fine. Of these 10,717, 1,670 were women and girls.

Speaking of their social relations, Mr. Felton's report says that 2,744 were married; 7,184 claimed to be single; 2,121 had children. It also shows that nearly 4,000 had no parents living; upward of 1,600 had only a mother living, and 822 had only a father living, showing that one half were without proper parental supervision.

Several years ago Mr. Fred L. Thompson, chaplain of the penitentiary at Chester, Illinois, made a personal inquiry of 500 convicts in regard to their early environment, and the result showed that 419, or upward of four-fifths, were parentless, or without proper home influence before reaching eighteen years of age. Also that 218 never had attended school. Mr. Thompson sums up an interesting report in these words: "I have come to the conclusion that there are two prime causes of crime; first, the want of proper home influence in childhood, and, second, the lack of thorough, well-disciplined training in early life." I will only add, it is the boy and girl who grow up on the streets or amid squalor and misery at home whose path seems forever to wind toward the prison door, and whatever system will train the youth, or will let light into the hovels, cellars, and garrets where children are growing up, will reduce the ranks of criminals.

The fact that all save ninety-six of the inmates of the bridewell for that year were there because they could not pay a fine, shows that they came from the poor, the very poor, the unfortunate. And as they had not been charged with any serious offense, and as the treatment which they got in the bridewell in twenty-six and one-tenth days would not build up or strengthen character, could not educate the mind or train the hand; and inasmuch as the treatment there, as in all prisons, of necessity tends to weaken self-respect, and as all these had to go out of the prison absolutely penniless and friendless—for they were sent there because they were penniless and friendless—I ask, What were these people to do when they came out? What could thy do to make an honest living? Take the 1,670 women and girls who were sent there because they had not the money with which to pay a small fine, and had not a friend upon earth to pay it for them; can any of you suggest what they could go at when they were turned out of the bridewell and found themselves on the corner of Twenty-sixth Street and California Avenue? There was absolutely nothing left for them except to go back to their old haunts—go anywhere where they could get something to eat and a night's lodging. And the prison experience they had had only degraded them, weakened them, and sank them lower into depravity.

The same may be said of the men and boys confined there. The city is full of men who have not been imprisoned, and who, during a large part of the year, can get nothing to do. It was estimated that this winter there were 60,000 men in Chicago out of employment. This being so, what show is there for a boy or a young man coming out of the bridewell to earn an honest living? And if imprisonment in the bridewell has not helped them, but, on the contrary, has, as a rule, injured them, wherein has society been benefited by the fact that it imprisoned 10,717 people on an average of twenty-six and one-tenth days, because they had committed trivial offenses? But some of you will ask, "Well, what have you to suggest? Society must be protected. We must preserve order." To which I reply, unquestionably society must be protected at all hazards, and we must preserve order and protect life and property. But I insist, to begin with, that it is unnecessary to arrest and lock up people who have committed no offense merely to preserve order; that the 15,000 who were not shown to have committed any offense in that year should never have been arrested and "run in" by the police; that arresting them neither tended to protect society nor to preserve order, but was a wrong—in many cases an outrage—for which society, in the end, must suffer; that the trouble is, that there has grown up in our police force a feeling that their efficiency is to be determined largely by the number of people they "run in," which is all wrong. Again, police officers too frequently feel that when they have arrested somebody, that it is then incumbent upon them to make a case against him, and hence are reckless in their swearing; so that it frequently happens that juries in criminal courts decline to give much credit to the testimony of a policeman. Policemen should fell that their standing is not to be determined by the number of people whom they may happen to arrest, but rather from their ability to preserve law and order; to protect life and property, by making but few arrests.

I am satisfied, further, that it would have been better if a great majority of the 28,000 who were fined in the police court had been let go, the offenses being so trivial that, in fact, it would have been better for society in the long run if no arrest at all had been made.

Then, in my judgment, we should adopt here a system which has been in operation in Massachusetts for over ten years, whereby the city is divided into districts, called probation districts, and in each district there is appointed a probation officer, whose duty it is to visit the prison every day in his district; get the name of the prisoner; go to his residence; see his family; acquaint himself, as far as is possible, with the history and character of the prisoner, his home influences and general environment, and if it is found that he is not vicious, and if the charge against him is not of such a heinous character as to require that he be confined, the probation officer recommends to the justice or to the judge, as the case may be, that if the accused is guilty, instead of sentence being pronounced, the case be continued from term to term; for the period of a year, sometimes more. This done, he is released; the probation officer assists him in getting employment, where this is practicable; assists him with counsel and advice; keeps a supervision over him for the period of a year, requiring him to report from time to time, and if he does not do well, the probation officer orders him arrested, and he is then sentenced.

This system has been in operation in Boston for upward of ten years. The city of Boston was divided, as I understand it, into three districts, and I have here the reports of the probation officers covering a period of ten years. In one district, during the year 1888, 1,139 prisoners were taken charge of by the probation officer. Of this number twelve ran away, or about one per cent.; fifty-two had to be surrendered, because they did not do well; but all the remainder did well—led sober and industrious lives. During ten years in one district 7,251 prisoners were taken charge of by the probation officer. Of this entire number, during the ten years, only 107 ran away, a very remarkable fact, which is to be borne in mind in considering the best method of dealing with people who have violated the law. Only a little over one per cent. ran away. Of the 7,251, 473 had to be returned for sentence. All the remainder did well. I will simply say that the results in the other probation districts of Boston were of the same character.

In speaking of the saving to both the prisoner and to society by this method of treatment, the officer reports that, had the lowest sentence possible been imposed, the aggregate time of all the prisoners which must have been spent in prison during the ten years would have amounted to 1,715 years, which was saved to society and to the accused, while the saving in expense to the public by not imprisoning amounted to many thousands of dollars per annum. The fact of having an intelligent and humane man acting as probation officer, visiting the home of the accused and assisting his family with counsel and advice, can scarcely be over-estimated; in many cases it will save not only the children, but also the parents from a criminal career. One of the probation officers of Boston, in speaking of those who were saved from imprisonment in his district, says: "Generally they have since lived good, orderly lives, and have been a blessing to their families, and where they were married, kept their homes from being broken up and their children from being sent to charitable institutions. In many cases they have changed from lives of vice and crime to become good citizens."

If we were to make our system what the law really intends it should be, and that is, protect society against crime, and would put a stop to the practice of arresting and breaking into prison experiences those who have been guilty of no offense, and would, further, put a stop to the practice of "running in" all who may have been guilty of some trivial offense, and would apply the Massachusetts system of probation in cases where the officer felt it could be safely done—for in many cases it could not be done—we would so greatly reduce the number who would have to be sent to prison that they could then be detained, not for twenty-six and one-tenth days in the bridewell, or from one to three years in the penitentiary, and not under the conditions that exist now in our prisons, where reformation and instruction are almost impossible; but they could be detained until, in the judgment of a competent board, the accused had acquired such habits of industry and had developed sufficient strength of character to go out and make his way in the world, and then he should be assisted in getting a position, so that he would not at once find himself penniless, friendless, and homeless. They should be sent to prison on an indeterminate sentence, nearly in accord with the system that has now for a number of years been in vogue in the Elmira prison in the State of New York, where prisoners must remain at least a year, and can be kept a number of years, if, in the judgment of the board, it is not safe to let them at large. Here prisoners go through a regular course of instruction, having regular hours of labor, and the treatment is of such a character as is calculated to develop and build up the man. And the management, instead of knowing nothing about the man, as is the case now with us, is put in possession of his whole history, all the information that can be gathered in regard to it, and whenever it becomes satisfied that the accused can with safety be given his liberty, the management first secures him employment, and exercises, for a period of at least six months, a sort of general supervision over him. If he does not do well they can take him back. If he loses his place they assist him in getting another; and if he does well for a period of a year he is discharged. And at different times men who have been discharged and then suddenly found themselves out of employment, rather than beg or steal voluntarily came back to the institution and asked to be taken in until they could get another job; and here, again, there were scarcely any desertions by those who were on parole.

Under such a system as this, hardened and dangerous criminals would not be set at liberty every two or three years, as they are now, to go out and prey upon society; but they would be kept confined until they could be safely set at liberty; while, on the other hand, the good intentioned who had got into trouble would not need to be confined behind brick walls until they became hardened, stolid, and desperate, as is now the case.

In addition to this, there should, in my judgment, be given every convict in prison an opportunity to earn something over and above the cost of keeping him. I know this involves difficulties, but none that cannot be overcome. He should be not only permitted to earn something, but he should be required to earn something to carry to his credit before he is again set at liberty; so that when he leaves the prison doors he will have something to sustain him for a while; and this should not be paid him at once, but in installments, so that he cannot lose it at once; or, if he has a family to support, he not only should be permitted to work, but required to earn something while in prison for the support of his family.

You will see, by such a system as I have outlined, the number whom we would have in the end to imprison would be greatly reduced; and these, too, could be so separated that the great majority could be set to work, if necessary, outside of the prison. They could farm; could be made to work the roads; could be made to do any kind of work, because the temptation to desert would then be practically taken away. I must say, however, that the temptation to desert is not so great at any time as many people suppose.

Major McClaughrey, who was for many years warden at the Joliet penitentiary, several years ago told me that he was then carrying on a small farm near the penitentiary, and working it with convicts, and they had had no trouble at all upon this point, and that he had repeatedly urged the State to buy him three or four hundred acres, and said if it would do so he could work the farm with the prisoners, and could raise not only what was needed for his institution, but for other State institutions, and that he had no fear at all of desertion.

If that is true at present, then under a system whereby the prisoner was made to feel that he was doing something for himself instead of simply wearing his life out for the benefit of some wealthy contractor, very little would need to be feared upon that point, and the number of prisoners who were serving long sentences, and who would be or were considered dangerous, and therefore have to be kept at work in the prison, would be so small by the time they were divided up among the various industries which are now carried on inside of the prison, the number in each industry would be so small that we would hear no more about prison-made goods coming in competition with free labor. The question of prison labor would solve itself.

We would thus save thousands of boys from a prison experience, and a possible criminal career. We would put an end to the practice of degrading and breaking down women and girls by repeated imprisonments for trivial offenses, which never does any good. We would prevent the really vicious and hardened criminals from being turned loose upon society every year or two. Both the convict and society would be the gainers.

INAUGURAL ADDRESS AS GOVERNOR OF ILLINOIS

Delivered at Springfield, January 10, 1893

In 1892 the time seemed ripe for a Democratic victory in Illinois. Populist fervor was sweeping the state, and Illinois Democrats, out of power for decades, sought a gubernatorial nominee who could command the loyalties of both urban workers and discontented farmers. They turned to John Peter Altgeld as their candidate. He was elected by a substantial margin, becoming the first foreign-born Governor of Illinois.

The rigors of the campaign brought on a physical breakdown, however, and it seemed for a time that he would not be able to take office. Nevertheless, Altgeld made the journey from Chicago to Springfield in order to attend the inauguration of the new state administration and to personally deliver his inaugural address before the Illinois Legislature. In this address, he outlined both the philosophy and the goals of his administration.

It has become the custom for each incoming Executive to deliver an inaugural address defining his position on public measures, and, to a limited extent, outlining the policy of the new administration. I shall follow this custom, although I realize that in this busy age comparatively few people pay any attention to inaugural addresses, but that both men and parties are judged by what they actually do, rather than by what they profess or promise. In order better to understand the present, we will glance for a moment at the past.

The policy of the State of Illinois was directed, almost wholly, by one of the great existing political parties, during the greater portion of the time from 1818, when it was admitted to the Union, until near the beginning of the civil war. This was the formative period, during which the foundations of our institutions were in great part laid, and those broad and liberal policies relating to education, internal improvements, the freedom of conscience and of speech, the rights of the citizens, the protection of property and the welfare of the masses, were not only adopted, but became so firmly rooted that their subsequent growth, as well as the development and greatness of the State, were assured. It was during this time that our common school system, the bulwark of free institutions, was founded and munificently endowed, in order that we might in time have the best schools in the world. During this time the State fostered a system of internal improvements, so as to encourage and hasten the development of our great natural resources. It not only caused the construction of a canal to connect the great lakes with the Mississippi system, but it encouraged the building of railroads so as to bring remote parts of the State close together. Notwithstanding its youth, Illinois then excelled almost every other State in that regard. At the same time the interests of the public were carefully guarded. It was during this period that an arrangement was made with the Illinois Central Railroad Company, in pursuance of which it now pays annually nearly half a million of dollars into the State treasury. Then came a change of party control, and soon thereafter the civil war. The young State, which had led in the development of civil institutions, took an equally patriotic and aggressive stand in favor of unholding the Union, and gave a greater per cent. of its population to carry on the war than almost any other State; and we now have a home for the aged heroes who were disabled in war, which is supported by the liberality of the State, and it will be our duty to see that this worthy object of a State's bounty is fairly and liberally treated.

The richness of our soil has attracted husbandmen from all quarters of the globe. Our great mineral resources and central location have drawn the manufacturers of almost every kind of goods; great railroads traverse nearly all parts of the State, while, owing to the push and enterprise of our people, our commercial interests are scarcely rivaled in the world. The present condition of our people, both in the State and in the Nation, is an illustration of the fact that in this country the people are greater than the government, and that they can attain a reasonable degree of prosperity and happiness in spite of unjust and injurious governmental policies. The recent action of our people at the polls is a warning that their patience has a limit, and that they cannot be long fed on empty and delusive promises. They demand of their servants that honesty and good faith which every employer has a right to expect at the hands of those who serve him.

Now, after an interval of more than thirty years, that political party which guided the councils of the State in its earlier history, again assumes control of its destinies, and we are confronted by a number of important problems, which for their proper solution, require painstaking investigation and deliberate judgment. These must all be treated by general laws, inasmuch as special legislation is not only prohibited by our Constitution, but it is antagonistic to democratic principles.

EDUCATION

Our great educational system is so well grounded that, with the exception of wasteful extravagance in some localities, it is working reasonably well. Its farther improvement will depend more upon the emulation of those who are laboring in that field, and their efforts to reach the highest degree of excellence, than it will upon legislation. But we have a statute, passed four years ago, known as the compulsory education act, which is no part of our common school system, and which violates the fundamental principles of free government. It will be our duty, not only to repeal this act at as early a day as practicable, but to provide in its place another law that shall be free from the objections that apply to this, and which shall make ample provisions for the care of neglected children. The State cannot permit children to grow up on the street, learning nothing but the rudiments of crime, and learning nothing to fit them for the discharge even of the ordinary duties of American citizenship, even that of self-maintenance.

PUBLIC FUNDS

The question as to who shall have the interest on public funds calls for the attention of the Legislature. While it may be true that the law does not contemplate that the funds shall be deposited at interest in banks, it is a notorious fact that all custodians of public funds actually draw interest on the balances of such funds. When the sums held were smaller, the matter attracted but little attention, but conditions have changed. The salary paid the custodians, whether of State, County, City, Park, School or other public funds, having been fixed when the amounts held were small, is now, in most cases, entirely disproportionate to the bond which has to be given and the responsibilities assumed; the custodian now obtaining, as a part of his compensation, the interest upon the public funds in his custody, but as this is in most cases many times as great as a reasonable compensation would be, the excess should belong to and be accounted for as part of the public funds; and inasmuch as the Constitution will not permit the salary of an official to be changed during his term of office, and as the terms of most of the custodians of public moneys, whether State, County, City, School, or other public funds, are brief, in my judgment the proper course will be to provide, by general law, that all such custodians that may hereafter be elected or appointed and qualified, shall be paid a salary to be determined by a per cent. of the amount of money they handle, and that all interest or increment earned by the fund in their possession, shall belong to the fund and be accounted for.

LIBERTY OF THE CITIZEN

Practically, there is at present neither Magna Charta nor Bill of Rights for the poor of our great cities. They have to submit to insult, assault and false imprisonment, and have no remedy, except a suit at law, which takes from three to five years, and requires time and money to prosecute; so they are practically without any remedy. Any man, rich or poor, taken into our higher courts, no matter on what charge, can have a jury trial and a full and fair hearing before sentence can be pronounced against him, but in the magistrate's court they deprive him of a jury trial by requiring him to advance the jury fee, which, when poor, he cannot do, so that he is compelled to submit to anything the magistrate may do, which frequently means anything that a police officer may wish to have done. In the city of Chicago, where there are a number of magistrates sitting at the same time, there are from thirty to fifty men and women tried by one magistrate in from one to two hours every day. The proceedings are not under the criminal laws as a rule, but fines are imposed, and when these are not promptly paid, imprisonment follows, just as it would in a case of conviction for crime in the higher court. While a judge of a higher court could not imprison a man for an hour without a jury trial, a simple magistrate actually does imprison scores every day without a jury trial.

During the year 1891, the police of Chicago alone arrested and carried to prison 70,550 people, including men, women and children. Of these, 32,500 were discharged by the magistrate, because, in most cases, no offense of any kind was proved; yet these people had been arrested, sometimes clubbed, taken through the streets in charge of officers, and sometimes kept in prison several days, just as if they were charged with murder; and all this not on any charge of crime, but generally at the mere discretion of some man wearing the uniform of law. When they finally got out they were practically without a remedy for the reason stated. Of the remaining 38,050, a little over 8,000 were sent to prison for various terms by the magistrates, because of their inability to pay the fines which had been imposed, and nearly all, except about ninety of these, were charged with trivial offenses, generally simply disorderly conduct. Yet their treatment was the same as if they had committed highway robbery, except that in the latter case they would have had something like a fair trial. The practice has long prevailed in Chicago and other cities, of raids being made by the police in the nighttime, and as many as a hundred or more men and women, sometimes only women, arrested and carried to prison in one night on no specific charge of crime, but simply at the caprice of a policeman. These cases have to be continued till the next morning. A bond is generally given, signed by a professional bailer. The justice charges a dollar for taking each bond, and the bailer all he can get for signing it, so that it is an exceedingly profitable business for those connected with the so-called police court.

While the law at present provides that nearly all other officers shall pay what fees they collect into the public treasury, and shall receive a salary for the services they render, this does not seem to apply to the magistrates. The law should be made more strict, and prohibit every officer, whether judicial or executive, who is in any way connected with the administration of justice, from keeping any fees under any pretext, for so long as he profits by the amount of business that is run in, there is a standing bribe to do injustice. The law should secure to all persons a fair jury trial before judgment can be pronounced by which they can be thrown into prison. These so-called raids neither prevent nor punish crime, but are simply irritants, and it is a notorious fact that real criminals frequently ply their vocation with great boldness at the very time that these raids are made, and they go uncaught and unpunished. On the other hand, there are many cases in which the police are rendered powerless to suppress crime by reason of political intrigue and interference. Our police system should be, so far as possible, placed beyond the reach of this character of interference.

I will also, in this connection, direct your attention to the fact that our system of administering justice in this State does not command the entire confidence of the public. This is due to the fact that, with our present machinery, litigation is so prolonged, and rendered so uncertain, without regard to the merits of the case, that many prudent men feel that they had better relinquish a claim and submit to an injustice than to venture into the courts. As a rule, the men who are directly occupied in the administration of justice in the higher courts of this State, are not only of the most able and learned, but of the highest character and unquestioned integrity. But the system is so defective that personal ability cannot overcome its deficiencies.

PUBLIC SERVICE

It will be our duty to endeavor to reduce the expense of the civil service of the State. There has been a tendency to create unnecessary boards, and, while some of these do not draw a salary, they are paid their expenses and a per diem, and they manage to draw large sums out of the State treasury. Many of these should be abolished, and their duties, so far as they perform any necessary service, be assigned to some of the regular County or State officers, who could attend to them without increased expense to the public. Again, the public service is frequently crowded by placing many more persons on the pay roll than are necessary to do the work. This not only increases the expenditure, but destroys the efficiency of the service. Whenever four men are set to do one man's work, no one of them will make an effort; all become careless, thoroughness will be lacking, and the result will be poor service. I desire to say a word in this connection in regard to the extraordinary demand for offices, both elective and appointive. While there are many men anxious to hold office for the honor of serving the people, and without reference to salary, there is no doubt that the demand is largely due to the fact that the applicants can get larger salaries while holding office than they can earn at the private employment for which they are qualified. The people of Illinois are willing to pay fair salaries for the service rendered, yet the question is worth considering, whether, if we were to reduce salaries, we would not get rid of the persistent demand for official positions, and at the same time increase the efficiency of the service. As the matter now stands, many capable but modest men who would gladly serve for a moderate salary are deterred from applying. It is a mistake to suppose that high salaries secure a higher grade of service to the public; if anything, they have the opposite effect. They give the office the character of spoils, and simply increase the endeavor to obtain it by men who want it for the money there is in it. In some States the experiment has been made by paying officials high salaries, and in none of them has the service been improved. While we must pay such salaries as will enable poor men to hold office, yet we must not lose sight of the fact that we get the highest grade of service from those men who esteem it an honor to serve the public, and with whom salaries are a secondary consideration.

Nearly all the great institutions of the State have, for years, been conducted on a partisan basis, and some of them rather offensively so. This has created a feeling of bitterness, and there is a widespread demand that there shall be a change in the management. There is also a belief that many of these institutions are extravagant and that their expenses are unnecessarily increased to accommodate political favorites. Inasmuch as it will be our duty to have them run in as economical a manner as possible, it will be necessary that those in charge shall be in thorough sympathy with the administration. Such changes as may be necessary should be made, care being taken to bring the service to the highest degree of excellence possible. I wish, however, in this connection, to submit that the time has come in the development of our great State when its public service should be, as far as possible, divorced from partisan politics, and when we should establish by law a classified civil service based upon honesty and capability, such as already prevails in some of the Eastern States. In all cases where the head officer is not directly responsible for the acts of his subordinates, such a civil service system should be established. This would apply to attendants in our State charitable and reformatory institutions and in the government of our cities.

CLAIMS OF LABOR

The State of Illinois already contains one of the greatest industrial communities in the world, and is rapidly growing. Not only are hundreds of millions of capital invested, but employment is given to hundreds of thousands of persons. The State must do justice to both employer and employe; it must see to it that law and order are maintained, and that life and property are thoroughly protected. Any weakness in this regard would be pusillanimous and invite incalculable evils. On the other hand, the State must not pursue such a policy as to convince the masses of the laboring people that the authority of the State is simply a convenient club for the use of the employer. When the State follows such a policy it forfeits the confidence of its people and itself sows the seed of anarchy. We must not forget that the law contemplates that the civil officer shall protect life and property, and for this purpose may order out the posse comitatus when necessary, and that a too hasty ordering out of the military creates irritation and bitterness, which frequently results in unnecessary bloodshed. Many civil officers have shown a disposition to shirk their duty during a strike, and this has been followed by the introduction of an irresponsible armed force controlled by private individuals. The presence of these armed strangers always acts as an irritation and tends to provoke riot and disorder, and we should take warning by the experience of some of our sister States and absolutely prohibit the use of these armed mercenaries by private corporations or individuals. At the same time we should see to it that the civil officers do their duty.

If we are to prosper we must make all of our people feel that the flag which floats over them is an emblem of justice. Our laboring people must either advance or retrograde. There is no such thing as standing still. If they are to advance, it must be by their own conservative and intelligent standing together. Only those forces survive which can take care of themselves. The moment individuals or classes become dependent they are objects of charity, and their case is then hopeless. If the laboring classes cannot thus stand together, they will be reduced to the condition of the laboring classes in the poorer countries of the old world. Such a condition would destroy the purchasing power of the American laborer, and with it destroy also the great American market. If ever the American laborer is reduced to that condition where he can buy only a little coarse clothing and a little amount of coarse food, the entire character of our institutions will be transformed, and the value of much of our manufacturing and railroad property depreciated.

STRIKES AND LOCKOUTS

The question of the protection of non-combatants—the great public—in the event of a strike or lockout, must not be over-looked in this connection. Conditions have so changed that it can no longer be said that it is nobody's business what other people do. All the elements of American society have become so interdependent, each class or interest has so adjusted itself to the other classes or interests, as to be in a measure dependent on them, and a suspension of the operation of one must injure the whole. For example, a strike on a railroad is not limited to a contention between employer and employe, but it affects all people along the line of the road who have adjusted their affairs to the operation of the road, and who are entitled to pro-tection at the hands of the State. Not only this, but when a large number of men are suddenly thrown out of employment, conditions are created which beget pauperism and crime and increase the burdens of the public. Especially is this true when an employer, who has so far interfered with the natural distribution of population as to cause a large number of men to settle where they would not otherwise have settled, suddenly attempts to discharge them all at once and to fill their places with others.

The reign of law has so broadened in this century as to cover almost every other controversy between man and man, and in the development of society some way must be found to subject the so-called "labor controversies" to law. This suggests the practicability of arbitration, and raises the question of the powers of the State in that regard. There seems to be no doubt about the right of the State to make a thorough investigation and render a decision, but the difficulty arises in enforcing the decision. The State cannot compel an unwilling employer to run his shop, nor can it compel unwilling employes to go to work. The State might compel an employer, who disregarded its decision and persisted in operating his works, to pay the expense of any special protection he received. On the other hand, if employes should refuse to go to work in accordance with the terms of a decision, the State can give its entire power in protecting the employer in hiring new men; but the moral influence alone of a State decision would, in many cases, be sufficient to end a strike, and some of the States have adopted laws creating Boards of Arbitration with this end in view, while others have gone further and attempted, in certain cases, to enforce the decisions of Boards of Arbitration. The constant increase in the use of labor-saving machinery tends to throw more and more men out of employment every year. This suggests the necessity of shortening the hours of labor, wherever this can be done by legislation, in order that all may still be able to get employment, and also that the working classes may derive some benefit from the great inventions of the age.

INSANE

While we already have erected four very large hospitals for the insane, still only about two-thirds of the insane of the State are properly cared for. Nearly one-third are in the poor-houses of the State, where they cannot be cared for, and exist in a horrible condition.

CHILD LABOR AND SANITATION

The increasing density of population in our large cities, and the establishment of what has been called "the sweating system," whereby many people are made to work amid sanitary conditions which constantly imperil the health of the community, and the employment of children in factories and shops, where they become stunted in both body and mind, and unfit for citizenship, call for more thorough legislation. Steps should also be taken to facilitate the work of furnishing proper homes in private families for dependent and neglected children.

MUNICIPAL POWERS

A number of large cities, both in this country and in Europe, have made the experiment of supplying their inhabitants with water, gas, electric light, and even operating the street railways, with very satisfactory results. I commend this subject to your careful consideration.

ROADS

While our State has developed in every other respect, we have made no progress in the matter of roads. We are, in this regard, almost where we were half a century ago, so that for a number of months in a year our roads are almost impassable. The loss and inconvenience of this falls most heavily on our agricultural communities. Not only is the farmer subjected to a heavy loss in the wear and tear of his team, but he is frequently prevented from availing himself of favorable markets by the impassableness of the roads. The State should again take up the subject of internal improvements, and adopt a policy that will tend to the building of good roads in every county in the State— roads that can be traveled every day in the year. As the railroads do all the carrying for long distances, wagon roads are, to a great extent, a local matter in each county. This being so, the roads will not need to be so wide, and can, therefore, be more cheaply built than would otherwise be possible. It is also probable that some of the convicts in our penitentiaries could be used to prepare material for the building of roads.

PENITENTIARIES

An amendment to the Constitution was adopted by the people in 1886, which prohibits the hiring of convict labor. This provision has been evaded and disregarded, and the affairs of the penitentiary have been so managed in the granting of space to the contractors as to make it difficult for the State to work prisoners on its own account. After the amendment was proposed, and in anticipation of its adoption, some contracts running for eight years were made. Although many other contracts had run out, these contracts have been presented as an excuse for the failure to enforce the command of the Constitution, but it has not been accepted as a valid one by the people. At the present time nearly all contracts have by their terms expired. The duty of the Legislature is plain. The convicts must be kept at work. A few of them could be set to preparing material for the making of roads, but other employment must be furnished for the remainder. Immediate action should be taken for the adoption of a plan for working convict labor consistent with the fundamental law I suggest that many industries be established, so as to interfere as little as possible with the markets and outside labor and industries. While this will require some considerable outlay for machinery and tools, there is no doubt that the penitentiaries can then, by proper management, be run without violating the law, without becoming a burden on the State, and without coming into ruinous competition with outside free labor.

PENAL LEGISLATION

In this connection I wish to call attention to the fact that, in the matter of penal legislation, our State is not abreast of the times. We still adhere to the old system of fixed sentences, under which the greatest inequality results; the vicious and hardened are frequently given short terms by a jury, while the comparatively innocent are given long terms by another jury. At best, first offenders and old criminals go in and out of prison together, while as a rule all classes come out without such training as will enable the individual to make a living, and utterly unable to find employment. Naturally these drift into a career of crime, and either prey upon the community or are returned to prison. Instead of this method, some of the States have adopted a system of indeterminate sentences, under which a prisoner is sentenced generally to the penitentiary, the law fixing the minimum and maximum time of imprisonment, and the actual length of confinement between these two points depends upon the general characteristics and personal conduct of the prisoner. Under this system the vicious and hardened can be restrained, while those who are comparatively innocent are released on parole, that is to say, on good behavior, but only after having been secured employment by the prison officials that will enable them to make an honest living. Under such a system, the number of convicts in our penitentiaries would be greatly reduced, and all problems involved in the treatment of criminals and the conduct of our penitentiaries more easily solved.

REDISTRICTING

The redistricting of the State will be one of the most important duties devolving upon this General Assembly. It will be difficult to so redistrict the State as to do exact justice to all interests and parties. Nevertheless, every effort should be made to come as near doing so as possible. As a rule, injustice benefits nobody, and almost invariably comes home to plague its authors.

TAXATION

Some of the States have tried the experiment of a heavy graduated succession tax on the estates of deceased persons. This has been followed with very satisfactory results. I commend this fact to your consideration; likewise the advisability of providing for a heavy corporation fee, to be paid at the organization of a corporation, as well as by all outside corporations coming here to do business. The practice of forming corporations to carry on the simple business affairs of life is becoming so common that a tax of this kind would be proper. Then, there is a wide-spread conviction that the present revenue system of our State results in the greatest inequalities and injustice in the matter of taxation. The subject is too great to be considered at present. Various measures in relation to it will no doubt be presented to your consideration, the most important of which is, perhaps, the question, whether any comprehensive change can be made without a revision of our constitution. In the past, our State has revised its constitution at intervals of thirty and twenty-two years.

A number of questions have arisen in the development of recent years, relating to various subjects on which legislation is needed, but where there seem to be constitutional difficulties in the way. This is especially true of the revenue system and of the question of enlarging the elective franchise, on which latter subject the law is left in a condition of uncertainty that is not creditable to the intelligence of our people. But I am aware that, as a rule, where so much is promised little is accomplished. I will, therefore, not go further into details. If I may be permitted to do so, I would like to suggest, for the consideration of the General Assembly, the propriety of making the sittings of the Legislature a little more continuous. A practice has grown up of working only a few days in the week. This not only tends to prolong the session, but necessitates constant interruption in the matter of considering any measure, and where this is the case, there cannot be that thorough examination of a subject that would otherwise be possible, and which is of the greatest importance as the preliminary of intelligent legislation.

REASONS FOR PARDONING FIELDEN, NEEBE, AND SCHWAB, THE SO-CALLED ANARCHISTS

Executive pardon issued at Springfield, June 26, 1893

When Altgeld took office as Governor of Illinois in January of 1893, no miscarriage of American justice loomed larger than the Haymarket Riot trial. Seven years earlier, there had been great labor unrest in Chicago, climaxed by a mass meeting in the Haymarket. Although the meeting had been peaceable, and in fact had begun to disperse, a formation of almost two hundred policemen prepared to attack the speakers and spectators. A bomb was thrown, and several policemen were killed. The police then opened fire upon the unarmed spectators.

Although it was impossible to determine who had thrown the bomb, eight Chicago labor leaders were tried on the ground that they had preached labor agitation and violence, and hence had incited the bomb-throwing. All were found guilty, and seven of them—Albert Parsons, August Spies, Samuel Fielden, Michael Schwab, George Engle, Adolph Fischer, and Louis Lingg—were sentenced to death. The eighth defendant, Oscar Neebe, was given a fifteen-year penitentiary sentence.

Many questions were raised about the legality of the trial; nevertheless, all judicial appeals failed. Fielden and Schwab then appealed for executive clemency, and Governor Oglesby—who privately shared the widespread misgivings about the trial—commuted their sentences to life imprisonment. On November 11, 1887, Parsons, Spies, Engle, and Fischer were hanged; Lingg escaped execution by committing suicide in his cell the day before.

When Altgeld took office, public opinion seemed prepared to accept a gubernatorial pardon of the three survivors, provided the pardon be made as an "act of mercy," without questioning the propriety of the trial. In discussing the case with associates and friends, Governor Altgeld held that the question of a pardon should rest upon whether or not the men were guilty as charged.

On June 26, 1893, Governor Altgeld exercised his power of executive clemency and, on the ground that they were illegally convicted, issued an unconditional pardon for the three surviving defendants, Fielden, Neebe, and Schwab.

STATEMENT OF THE CASE

On the night of May 4, 1886, a public meeting was held on Haymarket Square, in Chicago; there were from 800 to 1,000 people present, nearly all being laboring men. There had been trouble, growing out of the effort to introduce an eight-hour day, resulting in some collisions with the police, in one of which several laboring people were killed, and this meeting was called as a protest against alleged police brutality.

The meeting was orderly and was attended by the mayor, who remained until the crowd began to disperse, and then went away. As soon as Capt. John Bonfield, of the Police Department, learned that the mayor had gone, he took a detachment of police and hurried to the meeting for the purpose of dispersing the few that remained, and as the police approached the place of meeting a bomb was thrown by some unknown person, which exploded and wounded many and killed several policemen, among the latter being one Mathias Degan. A number of people were arrested, and after a time August Spies, Albert R. Parsons, Louis Lingg, Michael Schwab, Samuel Fielden, George Engle, Adolph Fischer, and Oscar Neebe were indicted for the murder of Mathias Degan. The prosecution could not discover who had thrown the bomb and could not bring the really guilty man to justice, and as some of the men indicted were not at the Haymarket meeting and had nothing to do with it, the prosecution was forced to proceed on the theory that the men indicted were guilty of murder, because it was claimed they had, at various times in the past, uttered and printed incendiary and seditious language, practically advising the killing of policemen, of Pinkerton men, and others acting in that capacity, and that they were, therefore, responsible for the murder of Mathias Degan. The public was greatly excited and after a prolonged trial all of the defendants were found guilty; Oscar Neebe was sentenced to fifteen years' imprisonment and all of the other defendants were sentenced to be hanged. The case was carried to the Supreme Court and was there affirmed in the fall of 1887. Soon thereafter Lingg committed suicide. The sentence of Fielden and Schwab was commuted to imprisonment for life; and Parsons, Fischer, Engle and Spies were hanged, and the petitioners now ask to have Neebe, Fielden and Schwab set at liberty.

The several thousand merchants, bankers, judges, lawyers and other prominent citizens of Chicago, who have by petition, by letter and in other ways urged executive clemency, mostly base their appeal on the ground that, assuming the prisoners to be guilty, they have been punished enough; but a number of them who have examined the case more carefully, and are more familiar with the record and with the fact disclosed by the papers on file, base their appeal on entirely different grounds. They assert:

First—That the jury which tried the case was a packed jury selected to convict.

Second—That according to the law as laid down by the Supreme Court, both prior to and again since the trial of this case, the jurors, according to their own answers, were not competent jurors, and the trial was, therefore, not a legal trial.

Third—That the defendants were not proven to be guilty of the crime charged in the indictment.

Fourth—That as to the defendant Neebe, the State's Attorney had declared at the close of the evidence that there was no case against him, and yet he has been kept in prison all these years.

Fifth—That the trial judge was either so prejudiced against the defendants, or else so determined to win the applause of a certain class in the community, that he could not and did not grant a fair trial.

Upon the question of having been punished enough, I will simply say that if the defendants had a fair trial, and nothing has developed since to show that they were not guilty of the crime charged in the indictment, then there ought to be no executive interference, for no punishment under our laws could then be too severe. Government must defend itself; life and property must be protected, and law and order must be maintained; murder must be punished, and if the defendants are guilty of murder, either committed by their own hands or by some one else acting on their advice, then, if they have had a fair trial, there should be in this case no executive interference. The soil of America is not adapted to the growth of anarchy. While our institutions are not free from injustice, they are still the best that have yet been devised, and therefore must be maintained.

WAS THE JURY PACKED?

I. The record of the trial shows that the jury in this case was not drawn in the manner that juries usually are drawn; that is, instead of having a number of names 'drawn out of a box that contained many hundred names, as the law contemplates shall be done in order to insure a fair jury and give neither side the advantage, the trial judge appointed one Henry L. Ryce as a special bailiff to go out and summon such men as he (Ryce) might select to act as jurors. While this practice has been sustained in cases in which it did not appear that either side had been prejudiced thereby, it is always a dangerous practice, for it gives the bailiff absolute power to select a jury that will be favorable to one side or the other. Counsel for the State, in their printed brief, say that Ryce was appointed on motion of defendants. While it appears that counsel for the defendants were in favor of having some one appointed, the record has this entry:

"Mr. Grinnell (The State's Attorney) suggested Mr. Ryce as special bailiff, and he was accepted and appointed." But it makes no difference on whose motion he was appointed if he did not select a fair jury. It is shown that he boasted while selecting jurors that he was managing this case; that these fellows would hang as certain as death; that he was calling such men as the defendants would have to challenge peremptorily and waste their challenges on, and that when their challenges were exhausted they would have to take such men as the prosecution wanted. It appears from the record of the trial that the defendants were obliged to exhaust all of their peremptory challenges, and they had to take a jury, almost every member of which stated frankly that he was prejudiced against them. On Page 133, of Volume I, of the record, it appears that when the panel was about two-thirds full, counsel for defendants called attention of the court to the fact that Ryce was summoning only prejudiced men, as shown by their examinations. Further: That he was confining himself to particular classes, i.e., clerks, merchants, manufacturers, etc. Counsel for defendants then moved the court to stop this and direct Ryce to summon the jurors from the body of the people; that is, from the community at large, and not from particular classes; but the court refused to take any notice of the matter.

For the purpose of still further showing the misconduct of Bailiff Ryce, reference is made to the affidavit of Otis S. Favor. Mr. Favor is one of the most reputable and honorable business men in Chicago, he was himself summoned by Ryce as a juror, but was so prejudiced against the defendants that he had to be excused, and he abstained from making any affidavit before sentence because the State's Attorney had requested him not to make it, although he stood ready to go into court and tell what he knew if the court wished him to do so, and he naturally supposed he would be sent for. But after the Supreme Court had passed on the case, and some of the defendants were about to be hanged, he felt that an injustice was being done, and he made the following affidavit:

STATE OF ILLINOIS, $\left.\right\}$ ss.
   Cook County.

Otis S. Favor, being duly sworn, on oath says that he is a citizen of the United States and of the State of Illinois, residing in Chicago, and a merchant doing business at Nos. 6 and 8 Wabash Avenue, in the city of Chicago, in said county. That he is very well acquainted with Henry L. Ryce, of Cook County, Illinois, who acted as special bailiff in summoning jurors in the case of The People, etc. vs. Spies et al., indictment for murder, tried in the Criminal Court of Cook county, in the summer of 1886. That affiant was himself summoned by said Ryce for a juror in said cause, but was challenged and excused therein because of his prejudice. That on several occasions in conversation between affiant and said Ryce touching the summoning of the jurors by said Ryce, and while said Ryce was so acting as special bailiff as aforesaid, said Ryce said to this affiant and to other persons in affiant's presence, in substance and effect as follows, to-wit: "I (meaning said Ryce) am managing this case (meaning this case against Spies et al.) and know what I am about. Those fellows (meaning the defendants, Spies et al.) are going to be hanged as certain as death. I am calling such men as the defendants will have to challenge peremptorily and waste their time and challenges. Then they

will have to take such men as the prosecution wants." That affiant
has been very reluctant to make any affidavit in this case, having
no sympathy with anarchy nor relationship to or personal interest in
the defendants or any of them, and not being a socialist, communist
or anarchist; but affiant has an interest as a citizen, in the due administration of the law, and that no injustice should be done under
judicial procedure, and believes that jurors should not be selected
with reference to their known views or prejudices. Affiant further says
that his personal relations with said Ryce were at said time, and for
many years theretofore had been most friendly and even intimate, and
that affiant is not prompted by any ill will toward any one in making
this affidavit, but solely by a sense of duty and a conviction of what
is due to justice.

Affiant further says, that about the beginning of October, 1886,
when the motion for a new trial was being argued in said cases before Judge Gary, and when, as he was informed, application was
made before Judge Gary for leave to examine affiant in open court,
touching the matters above stated, this affiant went, upon request
of State's Attorney Grinnell, to his office during the noon recess of
the court, and there held an interview with said Grinnell, Mr. Ingham
and said Ryce, in the presence of several other persons, including
some police officers, where affiant repeated substantially the matters
above stated, and the said Ryce did not deny affiant's statements, and
affiant said he would have to testify thereto if summoned as a witness, but had refused to make an affidavit thereto, and affiant was
then and there asked and urged to persist in his refusal and to make
no affidavit. And affiant further saith not.

OTIS S. FAVOR.

Subscribed and sworn to before me this 7th day of November, A.D.
1887.

JULIUS STERN,
Notary Public in and for said County.

So far as shown no one connected with the State's Attorney's
office has ever denied the statements of Mr. Favor, as to what
took place in that office, although his affidavit was made in
November, 1887.

As to Bailiff Ryce, it appears that he has made an affidavit
in which he denies that he made the statements sworn to by
Mr. Favor, but unfortunately for him, the record of the trial is
against him, for it shows conclusively that he summoned only the
class of men mentioned in Mr. Favor's affidavit. According to the
record, 981 men were examined as to their qualifications as
jurors, and most of them were either employers, or men who had
been pointed out to the bailiff by their employer. The following,

taken from the original record of the trial, are fair specimens of the answers of nearly all the jurors, except that in the following cases the court succeeded in getting the jurors to say that they believed they could try the case fairly notwithstanding their prejudices.

EXAMINATION OF JURORS

William Neil, a manufacturer, was examined at length; stated that he had heard and read about the Haymarket trouble, and believed enough of what he had so heard and read to form an opinion as to the guilt of the defendants, which he still entertained; that he had expressed said opinion, and then he added: "It would take pretty strong evidence to remove the impression that I now have. I could not dismiss it from my mind; could not lay it altogether aside during the trial. I believe my present opinion, based upon what I have heard and read, would accompany me through the trial, and would influence me in determining and getting at a verdict."

He was challenged by the defendants on the ground of being prejudiced, but the court then got him to say that he believed he could give a fair verdict on whatever evidence he should hear, and thereupon the challenge was overruled.

H. F. Chandler, in the stationery business with Skeen, Stuart & Co., said: "I was pointed out to the deputy sheriff by my employer to be summoned as a juror." He then stated that he had read and talked about the Haymarket trouble, and had formed and frequently expressed an opinion as to the guilt of the defendants, and that he believed the statements he had read and heard. He was asked:

Q. Is that a decided opinion as to the guilt of the defendants?
A. It is a decided opinion; yes, sir.
Q. Your mind is pretty well made up now as to their guilt or innocence?
A. Yes, sir.
Q. Would it be hard to change your opinion?
A. It might be hard; I cannot say. I don't know whether it would be hard or not.

He was challenged by the defendants on the ground of being prejudiced. Then the court took him in hand and examined him at some length, and got him to state that he believed he could try the case fairly. Then the challenge was overruled.

F. L. Wilson: Am a manufacturer. Am prejudiced and have formed and expressed an opinion; that opinion would influence me in rendering a verdict.

He was challenged for cause, but was then examined by the court.

Q. Are you conscious in your own mind of any wish or desire that there should be evidence produced in this trial which should prove some of these men, or any of them, to be guilty?

A. Well, I think I have.

Being further pressed by the court, he said that the only feeling he had against the defendants was based upon having taken it for granted that what he read about them was, in the main, true; that he believed that sitting as a juror the effect of the evidence either for or against the defendants would be increased or diminished by what he had heard or read about the case. Then on being still further pressed by the court, he finally said: "Well, I feel that I hope that the guilty one will be discovered or punished—not necessarily these men."

Q. Are you conscious of any other wish or desire about the matter than that the actual truth may be discovered?

A. I don't think I am.

Thereupon the challenge was overruled.

George N. Porter, grocer, testified that he had formed and expressed on opinion as to the guilt of the defendants, and that this opinion, he thought, would bias his judgment; he would try to go by the evidence, but that what he had read would have a great deal to do with his verdict; his mind, he said, was certainly biased now, and that it would take a great deal of evidence to change it. He was challenged for cause by the defendants; was examined by the court and said:

I think what I have heard and read before I came into court would have some influence with me. But the court finally got him to say he believed he could fairly and impartially try the case and render a verdict according to law and evidence, and that he would try to do so. Thereupon the court overruled the challenge for cause. Then he was asked some more questions by defendants' counsel, and among other things said:

Why, we have talked about it there a great many times and

I have always expressed my opinion. I believe what I have read in the papers; believe that the parties are guilty. I would try to go by the evidence, but in this case it would be awful hard work for me to do it.

He was challenged a second time on the ground of being prejudiced; was then again taken in hand by the court and examined at length, and finally again said he believed he could try the case fairly on the evidence; when the challenge for cause was overruled for the second time.

H. N. Smith, hardware merchant, stated among other things that he was prejudiced and had quite a decided opinion as to the guilt or innocence of the defendants; that he had expressed his opinion and still entertained it, and candidly stated that he was afraid he would listen a little more attentively to the testimony which concurred with his opinion than the testimony on the other side; that some of the policemen injured were personal friends of his. He was asked these questions:

Q. That is, you would be willing to have your opinion strengthened, and hate very much to have it dissolved?

A. I would.

Q. Under these circumstances do you think that you could render a fair and impartial verdict?

A. I don't think I could.

Q. You think you would be prejudiced?

A. I think I would be, because my feelings are very bitter.

Q. Would your prejudice in any way influence you in coming at an opinion, in arriving at a verdict?

A. I think it would.

He was challenged on the ground of being prejudiced; was interrogated at length by the court, and was brought to say he believed he could try the case fairly on the evidence produced in court. Then the challenge was overruled.

Leonard Gould, wholesale grocer, was examined at length; said he had a decided prejudice against the defendants. Among other things, he said: "I really don't know that I could do the case justice; if I was to sit on the case I should just give my undivided attention to the evidence and calculate to be governed by that." He was challenged for cause and the challenge overruled. He was then asked the question over again, whether he could render an impartial verdict based upon the evidence alone, that would be produced in court, and he answered: "Well, I answered that, as far as I could answer it."

Q. You say you don't know that you can answer that, either yes or no?

A. No, I don't know that I can.

Thereupon the court proceeded to examine him, endeavoring to get him to state that he believed he could try the case fairly upon the evidence that was produced in court, part of the examination being as follows:

Q. Now, do you believe that you can—that you have sufficiently reflected upon it—so as to examine your own mind, that you can fairly and impartially determine the guilt or innocence of the defendants?

A. That is a difficult question for me to answer.

Q. Well, make up your mind as to whether you can render, fairly and impartially render, a verdict in accordance with the law and the evidence. Most men in business possibly have not gone through a metaphysical examination so as to be prepared to answer a question of this kind.

A. Judge, I don't believe I can answer that question.

Q. Can you answer whether you believe you know?

A. If I had to do that I should do the best I could.

Q. The question is whether you believe you could or not. I suppose, Mr. Gould, that you know the law is that no man is to be convicted of any offense with which he is charged, unless the evidence proves that he is guilty beyond a reasonable doubt?

A. That is true.

Q. The evidence heard in this case in court?

A. Yes.

Q. Do you believe that you can render a verdict in accordance with the law?

A. Well, I don't know that I could.

Q. Do you believe that you can't—if you don't know of any reason why you cannot, do you believe that you can't.

A. I cannot answer that question.

Q. Have you a belief one way or other as to whether you can or can not? Not whether you are going to do it, but do you believe you can not? That is the only thing. You are not required to state what is going to happen next week or week after, but what do you believe about yourself, whether you can or can't?

A. I am about where I was when I started.

Some more questions were asked and Mr. Gould answered:

Well, I believe I have gone just as far as I can in reply to that question.

Q. This question, naked and simple in itself is, do you believe that you can fairly and impartially render a verdict in the case in accordance with the law and evidence?

A. I believe I could.

Having finally badgered the juror into giving this last answer, the court desisted. The defendants' counsel asked:

Do you believe you can do so, uninfluenced by any prejudice or opinion which you now have?

A. You bring it at a point that I object to and I do not feel competent to answer.

Thereupon the juror was challenged a second time for cause, and the challenge was overruled.

James H. Walker, dry goods merchant, stated that he had formed and expressed an opinion as to the guilt of defendants; that he was prejudiced, and stated that his prejudice would handicap him.

Q. Considering all prejudice and all opinions you have, if the testimony was equally balanced, would you decide one way or the other in accordance with that opinion of your prejudice?

A. If the testimony was equally balanced I should hold my present opinion, sir.

Q. Assuming that your present opinion is, that you believe the defendants guilty, would you believe your present opinion would warrant you in convicting them?

A. I presume it would.

Q. Well, you believe it would; that is your present belief, is it?

A. Yes, sir.

He was challenged on the ground of prejudice.

The court then examined him at length, and finally asked:

Q. Do you believe that you can sit here and fairly and impartially make up your mind, from the evidence, whether that evidence proves that they are guilty beyond a reasonable doubt or not?

A. I think I could, but I should believe that I was a little handicapped in my judgment, sir.

Thereupon the court, in the presence of the jurors not yet examined, remarked:

Well, that is a sufficient qualification for a juror in the case; of course, the more a man feels that he is handicapped the more he will be guarded against it.

W. B. Allen, wholesale rubber business, stated among other things:

Q. I will ask you whether what you have formed from what you have read and heard is a slight impression, or an opinion, or a conviction.

A. It is a decided conviction.

Q. You have made up your mind as to whether these men are guilty or innocent?

A. Yes, sir.

Q. It would be difficult to change that conviction, or impossible, perhaps?

A. Yes, sir.

Q. It would be impossible to change your conviction?

A. It would be hard to change my conviction.

He was challenged for cause by defendants. Then he was examined by the court at length and finally brought to the point of saying that he could try the case fairly and impartially, and would do so. Then the challenge for cause was overruled.

H. L. Anderson was examined at length, and stated that he had formed and expressed an opinion, still held it, was prejudiced, but that he could lay aside his prejudices and grant a fair trial upon the evidence. On being further examined, he said that some of the policemen injured were friends of his and he had talked with them fully. He had formed an unqualified opinion as to guilt or innocence of the defendants, which he regarded as deep-seated, a firm conviction that these defendants, or some of them, were guilty. He was challenged on the ground of prejudice, but the challenge was overruled.

M. D. Flavin, in the marble business. He had read and talked about the Haymarket trouble, and had formed and expressed an opinion as to the guilt or innocence of the defendants, which he still held and which was very strong; further, that one of the officers killed at the Haymarket was a relative of his, although the relationship was distant, but on account of this relationship his feelings were perhaps different from what they would have been, and occasioned a very strong opinion as to the guilt of the defendants, and that he had stated to others that he believed what he had heard and read about the matter. He was challenged on the ground of prejudice, and then stated, in answer to a question from the prosecution, that he believed that he could give a fair and impartial verdict, when the challenge was overruled.

Rush Harrison, in the silk department of Edson Keith & Co., was examined at length; stated that he had a deep-rooted conviction as to the guilt or innocence of the defendants. He said: "It would have considerable weight with me if selected as a juror. It is pretty deep-rooted, that opinion is, and it would take a large preponderance of evidence to remove it; it would require the preponderance of evidence to remove the opinion I now possess. I feel like every other good citizen does. I feel that these men are guilty; we don't know which; we have formed this opinion by general reports from the newspapers. Now, with that feeling, it would take some very positive evidence to make me think these men were not guilty, if I should acquit them; that is what I mean. I should act entirely upon the testimony; I would do as near as the main evidence would permit me to do. Probably I would take the testimony alone."

Q. But you say that it would take positive evidence of their innocence before you could consent to return them not guilty?

A. Yes, I should want some strong evidence.

Q. Well, if that strong evidence of their innocence was not introduced, then you want to convict them, of course?

A. Certainly.

He was then challenged on the ground of being prejudiced, when the judge proceeded to interrogate him and finally got him to say that he believed he could try the case fairly on the evidence alone; then the challenge was overruled.

J. R. Adams, importer, testified that he was prejudiced; had formed and expressed opinions and still held them. He was chal-

lenged on this ground, when the court proceeded to examine him
at length, and finally asked him this question:

Q. Do you believe that your convictions as to what the evidence proved, or failed to prove, will be at all affected by what
anybody at all said or wrote about the matter before?

A. I believe they would.

The court (in the hearing of other jurors not yet examined)
exclaimed: "It is incomprehensible to me." The juror was excused.

B. L. Ames, dealer in hats and caps stated that he was prejudiced; had formed and expressed opinions; still held them. He
was challenged on these grounds. Then the court examined him
at length; tried to force him to say that he could try the case
fairly, without regard to his prejudice, but he persisted in saying, in answer to the court's questions, that he did not believe
that he could sit as a juror, listen to the evidence and from that
alone make up his mind as to the guilt or innocence of the
defendants. Thereupon the court, in the presence of other jurors
not yet examined, lectured him as follows:

"Why not? What is to prevent your listening to the evidence
and acting alone upon it? Why can't you listen to the evidence
and make up your mind on it?

But the juror still insisted that he could not do it, and was
discharged.

H. D. Bogardus, flour merchant, stated that he had read and
talked about the Haymarket trouble; had formed and expressed
an opinion, still held it, as to the guilt or innocence of the defendants; that he was prejudiced; that this prejudice would certainly influence his verdict if selected a juror. "I don't believe
that I could give them a fair trial upon the proof, for it would
require very strong proof to overcome my prejudice. I hardly
think that you could bring proof enough to change my opinion."
He was challenged on the ground of prejudice.

Then the court took him in hand, and after a lengthy examination got him to say: "I think I can fairly and impartially render
a verdict in this case in accordance with the law and the evidence."

Then the challenge was overruled.

Counsel for defendants then asked the juror further questions, and he replied: "I say it would require pretty strong testimony to overcome my opinion at the present time; still, I think I could act independent of my opinion. I would stand by my opinion, however, and I think that the preponderance of proof would have to be strong to change my opinion. I think the defendants are responsible for what occurred at the Haymarket meeting. The preponderance of the evidence would have to be in favor of the defendants' innocence with me."

Then the challenge for cause was renewed, when the court remarked, in the presence of jurors not yet examined: "Every fairly intelligent and honest man, when he comes to investigate the question originally for himself, upon authentic sources of information, will, in fact, make his opinion from the authentic source, instead of hearsay that he heard before."

The court then proceeded to again examine the juror, and as the juror persisted in saying that he did not believe he could give the defendants a fair trial, was finally discharged.

These examinations are fair specimens of all of them, and show conclusively that Bailiff Ryce carried out the threat that Mr. Favor swears to. Nearly every juror called stated that he had read and talked about the matter, and believed what he had heard and read, and had formed and expressed an opinion, and still held it, as to the guilt or innocence of the defendants; that he was prejudiced against them; that that prejudice was deep-rooted, and that it would require evidence to remove that prejudice.

A great many said they had been pointed out to the bailiff by their employers, to be summoned as jurors. Many stated frankly that they believed the defendants to be guilty, and would convict unless their opinions were overcome by strong proofs; and almost every one, after having made these statements, was examined by the court in a manner to force him to say that he would try the case fairly upon the evidence produced in court, and whenever he was brought to this point he was held to be a competent juror, and the defendants were obliged to exhaust their challenges on men who declared in open court that they were prejudiced and believed the defendants to be guilty.

THE TWELVE WHO TRIED THE CASE

The twelve jurors whom the defendants were finally forced to accept, after the challenges were exhausted, were of the same general character as the others, and a number of them stated candidly that they were so prejudiced that they could not try the case fairly, but each, when examined by the court, was finally induced to say that he believed he could try the case fairly upon the evidence that was produced in court alone. For example:

Theodore Denker, one of the twelve: "Am shipping clerk for Henry W. King & Co. I have read and talked about the Haymarket tragedy, and have formed and expressed an opinion as to the guilt or innocence of the defendants of the crime charged in the indictment. I believe what I read and heard, and still entertain that opinion."

Q. Is that opinion such as to prevent you from rendering an impartial verdict in the case, sitting as a juror, under the testimony and the law?

A. I think it is.

He was challenged for cause on the ground of prejudice. Then the State's Attorney and the court examined him and finally got him to say that he believed he could try the case fairly on the law and the evidence, and the challenge was overruled. He was then asked further questions by the defendant's counsel, and said:

"I have formed an opinion as to the guilt of the defendants and have expressed it. We conversed about the matter in the business house and I expressed my opinion there; expressed my opinion quite frequently. My mind was made up from what I read and I did not hesitate to speak about it.

Q. Would you feel yourself in any way governed or bound in listening to the testimony and determining it upon the pre-judgment of the case that you had expressed to others before?

A. Well, that is a pretty hard question to answer.

He then stated to the court that he had not expressed an opinion as to the truth of the reports he had read, and finally stated that he believed he could try the case fairly on the evidence.

John B. Greiner, another one of the twelve: "Am a clerk for the Northwestern railroad. I have heard and read about the ·

killing of Degan, at the Haymarket, on May 4, last, and have formed an opinion as to the guilt or innocence of the defendants now on trial for that crime. It is evident that the defendants are connected with that affair from their being here."

Q. You regard that as evidence?

A. Well, I don't know exactly. Of course, I would expect that it connected them or they would not be here.

Q. So, then, the opinion that you now have has reference to the guilt or innocence of some of these men, or all of them?

A. Certainly.

Q. Now, is that opinion one that would influence your verdict if you should be selected as a juror to try the case?

A. I certainly think it would affect it to some extent; I don't see how it could be otherwise.

He further stated that there had been a strike in the freight department of the Northwestern road, which affected the department he was in. After some further examination, he stated that he thought he could try the case fairly on the evidence, and was then held to be competent.

G. W. Adams, also one of the twelve: "Am a traveling salesman; have been an employer of painters. I read and talked about the Haymarket trouble and formed an opinion as to the nature and character of the crime committed there. I conversed freely with my friends about the matter."

Q. Did you form an opinion at the time that the defendants were connected with or responsible for the commission of that crime?

A. I thought some of them were interested in it; yes.

Q. And you still think so?

A. Yes.

Q. Nothing has transpired in the interval to change your mind at all, I suppose.

A. No, sir.

Q. You say some of them; that is, in the newspaper accounts that you read, the names of some of the defendants were referred to?

A. Yes, sir.

After further examination he testified that he thought he could try the case fairly on the evidence.

H. T. Sanford, another one of the twelve: Clerk for the North-western railroad, in the freight auditor's office.

Q. Have you an opinion as to the guilt or innocence of the defendants of the murder of Mathias J. Degan?

A. I have.

Q. From all that you have heard and that you have read, have you an opinion as to the guilt or innocence of the defendants of throwing the bomb?

A. Yes, sir; I have.

Q. Have you a prejudice against socialists and communists?

A. Yes, sir, a decided prejudice.

Q. Do you believe that that prejudice would influence your verdict in this case?

A. Well, as I know so little about it, it is a pretty hard question to answer. I have an opinion in my own mind that the defendants encouraged the throwing of that bomb.

Challenged for cause on the ground of prejudice.

On further examination, stated he believed he could try the case fairly upon the evidence, and the challenge for cause was overruled.

Upon the whole, therefore, considering the facts brought to light since the trial, as well as the record of the trial and the answers of the jurors as given therein, it is clearly shown that, while the counsel for defendants agreed to it, Ryce was appointed special bailiff at the suggestion of the State's Attorney, and that he did summon a prejudiced jury which he believed would hang the defendants; and further, that the fact that Ryce was summoning only that kind of men was brought to the attention of the court before the panel was full, and it was asked to stop it, but refused to pay any attention to the matter, but permitted Ryce to go on, and then forced the defendants to go to trial before this jury.

While no collusion is proven between the judge and State's Attorney, it is clearly shown that after the verdict and while a motion for a new trial was pending, a charge was filed in court that Ryce had packed the jury, and that the attorney for the State got Mr. Favor to refuse to make an affidavit bearing on this point, which the defendants could use, and then the court refused to take any notice of it unless the affidavit was obtained, although it was informed that Mr. Favor would not make an affidavit, but stood ready to come into court and make a full statement if the court desired him to do so.

These facts alone would call for executive interference, especially as Mr. Favor's affidavit was not before the Supreme Court at the time it considered the case.

RECENT DECISION OF THE SUPREME COURT
AS TO THE COMPETENCY OF JURORS

II. The second point argued seems to me to be equally conclusive. In the case of the People vs. Coughlin, known as the Cronin case, recently decided, the Supreme Court, in a remarkably able and comprehensive review of the law on this subject, says, among other things:

"The holding of this and other courts is substantially uniform, that where it is once clearly shown that there exists in the mind of the juror, at the time he is called to the jury box, a fixed and positive opinion as to the merits of the case, or as to the guilt or innocence of the defendant he is called to try, his statement that, notwithstanding such opinion, he can render a fair and impartial verdict according to the law and evidence, has little, if any, tendency to establish his impartiality. This is so because the juror who has sworn to have in his mind a fixed and positive opinion as to the guilt or innocence of the accused, is not impartial, as a matter of fact. . . .

"It is difficult to see how, after a juror has avowed a fixed and settled opinion as to the prisoner's guilt, a court can be legally satisfied of the truth of his answer that he can render a fair and impartial verdict, or find therefrom that he has the qualification of impartiality, as required by the Constitution. . . .

"Under such circumstances, it is idle to inquire of the jurors whether they can return just and impartial verdicts. The more clear and positive were their impressions of guilt, the more certain they may be that they can act impartially in condemning the guilty party. They go into the box in a state of mind that is well calculated to give a color of guilt to all the evidence, and if the accused escapes conviction, it will not be because the ecidence has not established guilt beyond a reasonable doubt, but because an accused party condemned in advance, and called upon to exculpate himself before a prejudiced tribunal, has succeeded in doing so.

"To try a cause by such a jury is to authorize men, who state that they will lean in their finding against one of the parties, unjustly to determine the rights of others, and it will be no difficult task to predict, even before the evidence was heard, the verdict that would be rendered. Nor can it be said that instructions from the court would correct the bias of the jurors who swear they incline in favor of one of the litigants. . . .

"Bontecou (one of the jurors in the Cronin case), it is true, was brought to make answer that he could render a fair and impartial verdict in accordance with the law and the evidence, but that result was reached only after a singularly argumentative and persuasive cross-examination by the court, in which the right of every person accused of crime to an impartial trial and to the presumption of innocence until proved guilty beyond a reasonable doubt, and the duty of every citizen, when summoned as a juror, to lay aside all opinions and prejudices and accord the accused such a trial, was set forth and descanted upon at length, and in which the intimation was very clearly made that a juror who could not do this was recreant to his duty as a man and a citizen. Under pressure of this sort of cross-examination, Bontecou seems to have been finally brought to make answer in such a way as to profess an ability to sit as an impartial juror, and on his so answering he was pronounced competent and the challenge as to him was overruled. Whatever may be the weight ordinarily due to statements of this character by jurors, their value as evidence is in no small degree impaired in this case by the mode in which they were, in a certain sense, forced from the mouth of the juror. The theory seemed to be that if a juror could in any way be brought to answer that he could sit as an impartial juror, that declaration of itself rendered him competent. Such a view, if it was entertained, was a total misconception of the law. . . .

"It requires no profound knowledge of human nature to know that with ordinary men opinions and prejudices are not amenable to the power of the will, however honest the intention of the party may be to put them aside. They are likely to remain in the mind of the juror in spite of all his efforts to get rid of them, warping and giving direction to his judgment, coloring the facts as they are developed by the evidence, and exerting an influence more or less potent, though it be unconsciously to the juror himself, on the final result of his deliberations. To compel a person accused of a crime to be tried by a juror who has prejudiced his case is not a fair trial. Nor should a defendant be compelled to rely, as his security for the impartiality of the jurors by whom he is to be tried, upon the restraining and controlling influence upon the juror's mind of his oath to render a true verdict according to the law and the evidence. His impartiality should appear before he is permitted to take the oath. If he is not impartial then, his oath cannot be relied upon to make him so. In the terse and expressive language of Lord Coke, already quoted, the jury should 'stand indifferent as he stands unsworn'."

Applying the law as here laid down in the Cronin case to the answers of the jurors above given in the present case, it is very apparent that most of the jurors were incompetent because they were not impartial, for nearly all of them candidly stated that they were prejudiced against the defendants, and believed them guilty before hearing the evidence, and the mere fact that the judge succeeded, by a singularly suggestive examination, in getting them to state that they believed they could try the case fairly on the evidence, did not make them competent.

It is true that this case was before the Supreme Court, and that court allowed the verdict to stand; and it is also true that in the opinion of the majority of the court in the Cronin case, an effort is made to distinguish that case from this one; but it is evident that the court did not have the record of this case before it when it tried to make the distinction, and the opinion of the minority of the court in the Cronin case expressly refers to this case as being exactly like that one, so far as relates to the competency of the jurors. The answers of the jurors were almost identical and the examinations were the same. The very things which the Supreme Court held to be fatal errors in the Cronin case, constituted the entire fabric of this case, so far as relates to the competency of the jury. In fact, the trial judge in the Cronin case was guided by the rule laid down in this case, yet the Supreme Court reversed the Cronin case because two of the jurors were held to be incompetent, each having testified that he had read and talked about the case, and had formed and expressed an opinion as to the guilt of the defendants; that he was prejudiced; that he believed what he had read, and that his prejudice might influence his verdict; that his prejudice amounted to a conviction on the subject of the guilt or innocence of the defendants; but each finally said that he could and would try the case fairly on the evidence alone, etc.

A careful comparison of the examination of these two jurors with that of many of the jurors in this case, shows that a number of the jurors in this case expressed themselves, if anything, more strongly against the defendants than these two did; and what is still more, one of those summoned, Mr. M. D. Flavin, in this case, testified not only that he had read and talked about the case, and had formed and expressed an opinion as to the guilt or innocence of the defendants, that he was bitterly prejudiced, but further, that he was related to one of the men who was killed, and that for that reason he felt more strongly against the defendants than he otherwise might, yet he was held to be competent on his mere statement that he believed he could try the case fairly on the evidence.

No matter what the defendants were charged with, they were entitled to a fair trial, and no greater danger could possibly threaten our institutions than to have the courts of justice run wild or give way to popular clamor; and when the trial judge in this case, ruled that a relative of one of the men who was killed was a competent juror, and this after the man had candidly stated that he was deeply prejudiced, and that his relationship caused him to feel more strongly than he otherwise might; and when, in scores of instances, he ruled that men who candidly declared that they believed the defendants to be guilty, that this was a deep conviction and would influence their verdict, and that it would require strong evidence to convince them that the defendants were innocent; when in all these instances the trial judge ruled that these men were competent jurors, simply because they had, under his adroit manipulation, been led to say that they believed they could try the case fairly on the evidence, then the proceedings lost all semblance of a fair trial.

DOES THE PROOF SHOW GUILT?

III. The State has never discovered who it was that threw the bomb which killed the policeman, and the evidence does not show any connection whatever between the defendants and the man who did throw it. The trial judge, in overruling the motion for a new hearing, and again, recently in a magazine article, used this language:

"The conviction has not gone on the ground that they did have actually any personal participation in the particular act which caused the death of Degan, but the conviction proceeds upon the ground that they had generally, by speech and print, advised large classes of the people, not particular individuals, but large classes, to commit murder, and had left the commission, the time and place and when, to the individual will and whim or caprice, or whatever it may be, of each individual man who listened to their advice, and that in consequence of that advice, in pursuance of that advice, and influenced by that advice, somebody not known did throw the bomb that caused Degan's death. Now, if this is not a correct principle of the law, then the defendants of course are entitled to a new trial. This case is without a precedent; there is no example in the law books of a case of this sort."

The judge certainly told the truth when he stated that this case was without a precedent, and that no example could be found in the law books to sustain the law as above laid down. For, in all the centuries during which government has been maintained among men, and crime has been punished, no judge in a civilized country has ever laid down such a rule before. The petitioners claim that it was laid down in this case simply because the prosecution, not having discovered the real criminal, would otherwise not have been able to convict anybody; that this course was then taken to appease the fury of the public, and that the judgment was allowed to stand for the same reason. I will not discuss this. But taking the law as above laid down, it was necessary under it to prove, and that beyond a reasonable doubt, that the person committing the violent deed had at least heard or read the advice given to the masses, for until he either heard or read it he did not receive it, and if he did not receive it, he did not commit the violent act in pursuance of that advice; and it is here that the case for the State fails; with all his apparent eagerness to force conviction in court, and his efforts in defending his course since the trial, the judge, speaking on this point in his magazine article, makes this statement: "It is probably true that Rudolph Schnaubelt threw the bomb," which statement is merely a surmise and is all that is known about it, and is certainly not sufficient to convict eight men on. In fact, until the State proves from whose hands the bomb came, it is impossible to show any connection between the man who threw it and these defendants.

It is further shown that the mass of matter contained in the record and quoted at length in the judge's magazine article, showing the use of seditious and incendiary language, amounts to but little when its source is considered. The two papers in which articles appeared at intervals during years, were obscure little sheets, having scarcely any circulation, and the articles themselves were written at times of great public excitement, when an element in the community claimed to have been outraged; and the same is true of the speeches made by the defendants and others; the apparently seditious utterances were such as are always heard when men imagine that they have been wronged, or are excited or partially intoxicated; and the talk of a gigantic anarchistic conspiracy is not believed by the then Chief of Police, as will be shown hereafter, and it is not entitled to serious notice, in view of the fact that, while Chicago had nearly a million inhabitants, the meetings held on the lake front on Sundays during the summer, by these agitators, rarely had fifty people present, and most of these went from mere curiosity, while the meetings held in-doors, during the winter, were still smaller. The meetings held from time to time by the masses of the laboring people, must not be confounded with the meetings above named, although in times of excitement and trouble much violent talk was indulged in by irresponsible parties; which was forgotten when the excitement was over.

Again, it is shown here that the bomb was, in all probability, thrown by some one seeking personal revenge; that a course had been pursued by the authorities which would naturally cause this; that for a number of years prior to the Haymarket affair there had been labor troubles, and in several cases a number of laboring people, guilty of no offense, had been shot down in cold blood by Pinkerton men, and none of the murderers were brought to justice. The evidence taken at coroners' inquests and presented here, shows that in at least two cases men were fired on and killed when they were running away, and there was consequently no occasion to shoot, yet nobody was punished; that in Chicago there had been a number of strikes in which some of the police not only took sides against the men, but without any authority of law invaded and broke up peaceable meetings, and in scores of cases brutally clubbed people who were guilty of no offense whatever. Reference is made to the opinion of the late Judge McAllister, in the case of the Harmonia Association of Joiners against Brenan, et al., reported in the Chicago Legal News. Among other things, Judge McAllister says:

"The facts established by a large number of witnesses, and without any opposing evidence, are, that this society, having leased Turner Hall, on West Twelfth street, for the purpose, held a meeting in the forenoon of said day, in said hall, composed of from 200 to 300 individuals, most of whom were journeymen cabinet-makers engaged in the several branches of the manufacture of furniture in Chicago, but some of those in attendance were the proprietors in that business, or the delegates sent by them. The object of the meeting was to obtain a conference of the journeymen with such proprietors, or their authorized delegates, with a view of endeavoring to secure an increase of the price or diminution of the hours of labor. The attendants were wholly unarmed, and the meeting was perfectly peaceable and orderly, and while the people were sitting quietly, with their backs toward the entrance hall, with a few persons on the stage in front of them, and all engaged merely in the business for which they had assembled, a force of from fifteen to twenty policemen came suddenly into the hall, having a policeman's club in one hand and a revolver in the other, and making no pause to determine the actual character of the meeting, they immediately shouted: "Get out of here, you damned sons-of-bitches," and began beating the people with their clubs, and some of them actually firing their revolvers. One young man was shot through the back of the head and killed. But to complete the atrocity of the affair on the part of the officers engaged in it, when the people hastened to make their escape from the assembly room, they found policemen stationed on either side of the stairway leading from the hall down to the street, who applied their clubs to them as they passed, seemingly with all the violence practicable under the circumstances.

"Mr. Jacob Beiersdorf, who was a manufacturer of furniture, employing some 200 men, had been invited to the meeting and came, but as he was about to enter the place where it was held, an inoffensive old man, doing nothing unlawful, was stricken down at his feet by a policeman's club.

"These general facts were established by an overwhelming mass of testimony, and for the purpose of the questions in the case, it is needless to go farther into detail.

"The chief political right of the citizen in our government, based upon the popular will as regulated by law, is the right of suffrage, but to that right two others are auxiliary and of almost equal importance:

"First. The right of free speech and of a free press.

"Second. The right of the people to assemble in peaceable manner to consult for the common good.

"These are among the fundamental principles of government and guaranteed by our Constitution. Section 17, article 2, of the bill of rights, declares: 'The people have a right to assemble in a peaceable manner to consult for the common good, to make known their opinions to their representatives, and apply for redress of grievances.' Jurists do not regard these declarations of the bill of rights as creating or conferring the rights, but as a guarantee against their deprivation or infringement by any of the powers or agencies of the Government. The rights themselves are regarded as the natural inalienable rights belonging to every individual, or as political, and based upon or arising from principles inherent in the very nature of a system of free government.

"The right of the people to assemble in a peaceable manner to consult for the common good, being a Constitutional right, it can be exercised and enjoyed within the scope and the spirit of that provision of the Constitution, independently of every other power of the State Government.

"Judge Cooley, in his excellent work on 'Torts,' speaking (p. 296) of remedies for the invasion of political rights, says: 'When a meeting for any lawful purpose is actually called and held, one who goes there with the purpose to disturb and break it up, and commits disorder to that end, is a trespasser upon the rights of those who, for a time, have control of the place of meeting. If several unite in the disorder it may be a criminal riot.' "

So much for Judge McAllister.

Now, it is shown that no attention was paid to the Judge's decision; that peaceable meetings were invaded and broken up, and inoffensive people were clubbed; that in 1885 there was a strike at the McCormick Reaper Factory, on account of a reduction of wages, and some Pinkerton men, while on their way there, were hooted at by some people on the street, when they fired into the crowd and fatally wounded several people who had taken no part in any disturbance; that four of the Pinkerton men were indicted for this murder by the grand jury, but that the prosecuting officers apparently took no interest in the case, and allowed it to be continued a number of times, until the witnesses were sworn out, and in the end the murderers went free; that after this there was a strike on the West Division Street railway, and that some of the police, under the leadership of Capt. John Bonfield, indulged in a brutality never equalled before; that even small merchants, standing on their own doorsteps and having no interest in the strike, were clubbed then hustled into patrol wagons, and thrown into prison on no charge and not even booked; that a petition signed by about 1,000 of the leading citizens living on and near West Madison street, was sent to the Mayor and City Council, praying for the dismissal of Bonfield from the force, but that, on account of his political influence, he was retained. Let me say here, that the charge of brutality does not apply to all of the policemen of Chicago. There are many able, honest and conscientious officers who do their duty quietly, thoroughly and humanely.

As a specimen of the many papers filed in this connection, I will give the following, the first being from the officers of a corporation that is one of the largest employers in Chicago:

Office People's Gas Light and Coke Co.,
Chicago, Nov. 21, 1885.

To the Chairman of the Committee, Chicago Trades and
Labor Assembly:

Sir: In response to the request of your committee for information
as to the treatment received by certain employes of this company
at the hands of Captain Bonfield, and by his orders, during the strike
of the Western Division Railway Company's employes in July last,
you are advised as follows:

On that day of the strike, in which there was apparently an indiscriminate arresting of persons who happened to be up on Madison
street, whether connected with the disturbance of the peace or engaged in legitimate business, a number of employes of this company
were at work upon said street, near Hoyne avenue, opening a trench
for the laying of gas pipe.

The tool box of the employes was at the southeast corner of Hoyne
and Madison street. As the men assembled for labor, shortly before
7 a.m., they took their shovels and tools from the tool box, arranged
themselves along the trench preparatory to going to work when the
hour of seven should arrive. About this time, and a little before the
men began to work, a crowd of men, not employes of this company,
came surging down the street from the west, and seizing such shovels
and other tools of the men as lay upon the ground and about the
box, threw more or less of the loose dirt, which before had been
taken from the trench, upon the track of the railway company. About
this time Captain Bonfield and his force appeared upon the scene,
and began apparently an indiscriminate arrest of persons. Among
others arrested were the following employes of this company: Edward
Kane, Mike W. Kerwin, Dan Diamond, Jas. Hussey, Dennis Murray,
Patrick Brown and Pat Franey. No one of these persons had any
connection with the strike, or were guilty of obstructing the cars of
the railway company, or of any disturbance upon the street. Mr.
Kerwin had just arrived at the tool box and had not yet taken his
shovel preparatory to going to work, when he was arrested while
standing by the box, and without resistance was put upon a street
car as prisoner. When upon the car he called to a friend among the
workmen, saying: "Take care of my shovel." Thereupon Bonfield
struck him a violent blow with a club upon his head, inflicting a
serious wound, laying open his scalp, and saying as he did so: "I
will shovel you," or words to that effect. Another of the said employes,
Edward Kane, was also arrested by the tool box, two of the police
seizing him, one by each arm, and as he was being put upon the car,
a third man, said by Kane and others to be Bonfield, struck him
with a club upon the head, severely cutting his head. Both of these
men were seriously injured, and for a time disabled from attending to
their business. Both of these men, with blood streaming from cuts
upon their heads, respectively, as also were all of the others above
named, were hustled off to the police station and locked up. The men

were not "booked" as they were locked up, and their friends had great difficulty in finding them, so that bail might be offered and they released. After they were found communication with them was denied for some time, by Bonfield's orders it was said, and for several hours they were kept in confinement in the lock-up upon Desplaines street, as criminals, when their friends were desirous in bailing them out. Subsequently they were all brought up for trial before Justice White. Upon the hearing the city was represented by its attorney, Bonfield himself being present, and from the testimony it appeared that all these men had been arrested under the circumstances aforesaid, and without the least cause, and that Kane and Kerwin had been cruelly assaulted and beaten without the least justification therefor, and, of course, they were all discharged.

The officers of this company, who are cognizant of the outrages perpetrated upon these men, feel that the party by whom the same were committed ought not to remain in a responsible position upon the police force.

PEOPLE'S GAS LIGHT AND COKE CO.,

By C. K. G. Billings, V.P.

ROBERT ELLIS, 974 West Madison Street:

Chicago, Nov. 19, 1885.

I kept a market at 974 West Madison Street. I was in my place of business waiting on customers, and stepped to the door to get a measure of vegetables. The first thing I knew, as I stood on the step in front of my store, I received a blow over the shoulders with a club, and was seized and thrown off the sidewalk into a ditch being dug there. I had my back to the person who struck me, but on regaining my feet I saw that it was Bonfield who had assaulted me. Two or three officers then came up. I told them not to hit me again. They said go and get in the car, and I told them that I couldn't leave my place of business as I was all alone there. They asked Bonfield and he said, "Take him right along." They then shoved me into the car and took me down the street to a patrol wagon, in which I was taken to the Lake street station. I was locked up there from this time, about eight o'clock in the morning, till eight o'clock in the evening, and then taken to the Desplaines street station. I was held there a short time and then gave bail for my appearance, and got back to my place of business about nine o'clock at night. Subsequently, when I appeared in court, I was discharged. It was about eight o'clock in the morning, July 3, 1885, when I was taken from my place of business.

ROBERT ELLIS.

W. W. WYMAN, 1004 West Madison Street:

Chicago, Nov. 19, 1885.

I was standing in my door about seven o'clock in the morning of July 3, 1885. I saw a man standing on the edge of the sidewalk. He wasn't doing anything at all. Bonfield came up to him and without a word being said by either, Bonfield hit him over the head with his club and knocked him down. He also hit him twice after he had fallen. I was standing about six feet from them when the assault oc· curred. I don't know the man that was clubbed—never saw him before nor since.

W. W. WYMAN.

JESSE CLOUD, 998 Monroe Street:

Chicago, Nov. 20, 1885.

On the morning of July 3, 1885, about seven o'clock, as I was standing on the southeast corner of Madison street and Western avenue, I saw Bonfield walk up to a man on the opposite corner, who was apparently looking at what was going on in the street. Bonfield hit him over the head with his club and knocked him down. Some men who were near him helped him over to the drug store on the corner where I was standing. His face was covered with blood from the wound on his head, made by Bonfield's club, and he appeared to be badly hurt. A few moments later, as I was standing in the same place, almost touching elbows with another man, Bonfield came up facing us, and said to us, "stand back," at the same time striking the other man over the head with his club. I stepped back and turned around to look for the other man; saw him a few feet away with the blood running down over his face, apparently badly hurt from the effect of the blow or blows he had received from Bonfield. There was no riot or disorderly conduct there at the time, except what Bonfield made himself by clubbing innocent people, who were taking no part in the strike. If they had been there for the purpose of rioting they would surely have resisted Bonfield's brutality.

I affirm that the above statement is a true and correct statement of facts.

JESSE CLOUD.

H. J. NICHOLS, 47 Flournoy Street:

Chicago, Nov. 19, 1885.

On the morning of July 3, 1885, I was driving up Madison street, just coming from Johnson's bakery, on Fifth avenue. When I got to the corner of Market and Madison streets, I met the cars coming over the bridge. On looking out of my wagon I saw Bonfield by the side of a car. He snatched me from my wagon and struck me on the head, cutting it open, and put me in a car, leaving my wagon standing there unprotected, loaded with bakery goods, all of which were stolen, except a few loaves of bread. I was taken to the Desplaines street station and locked up for about ten hours. I was then bound over for riot, in $500 bail, and released. During the time I was there I received no attention of any kind, though by head was seriously cut.

Julius Goldzier, my lawyer, went to Bonfield with me before the case was called into court, and told him I had done nothing, and Bonfield said, "scratch his name off," and I was released.
I swear to the truth of the above.

H. J. NICHOLS.

The following is from Capt. Schaack, a very prominent police official:

Department of Police,
City of Chicago.
Chicago, Illinois, May 4, 1893.

Mr. G. E. Detwiler, Editor Rights of Labor:

Dear Sir: In reply to your communication of April 13, I will say that in July, 1885, in the street car strike on the West Side, I held the office of lieutenant on the force. I was detailed with a company of officers, early in the morning, in the vicinity of the car barns, I believe on Western avenue and a little north of Madison street. My orders were to see that the new men on the cars were not molested when coming out of the barns.

One man came out and passed my lines about fifty feet. I saw one of the men, either driver or conductor, leave the car at a stand-still. I ran up near the car, when I saw, on the southeast corner of the street, Bonfield strike a man on the head with his club. He hit the man twice and I saw the man fall to the ground.

Afterwards I was put on a train of cars, protecting the rear. Bonfield had charge of the front. I saw many people getting clubbed in front of the train, but I held my men in the rear and gave orders not to strike anyone except they were struck first. Not one of my officers hurt a person on that day or at any time.

Many people were arrested, all appearing. From what I saw in the afternoon and the next day, no officer could state what they were arrested for. The officers professed ignorance of having any evidence, but "some one told them to take him in," meaning to lock him up. On that afternoon, about four o'clock, I met Bonfield and he addressed me in the following words, in great anger: "If some of you goody-goody fellows had used your clubs freely in the forenoon, you would not need to use lead this afternoon." I told him that I did not see any use in clubbing people, and that I would club no person to please any one, meaning Bonfield; and that if lead had to be used, I thought my officers could give lead and take it also. I will say that affair was brutal and uncalled for.

MICHAEL J. SCHAACK,
227 N. State Street.

Again, it is shown that various attempts were made to bring to justice the men who wore the uniform of the law while violating it, but all to no avail; that the laboring people found the prisons always open to receive them, but the courts of justice were practically closed to them; that the prosecuting officers vied with each other in hunting them down, but were deaf to their appeals; that in the spring of 1886 there were more labor disturbances in the city, and particularly at the McCormick factory; that under the leadership of Capt. Bonfield the brutalities of the previous year were even exceeded. Some affidavits and other evidence is offered on this point, which I cannot give for want of space. It appears that this was the year of the eight-hour agitation, and efforts were made to secure an eight-hour day about May 1, and that a number of laboring men standing, not on the street, but on a vacant lot, were quietly discussing the situation in regard to the movement, when suddenly a large body of police, under orders from Bonfield, charged on them and began to club them; that some of the men, angered at the unprovoked assault, at first resisted, but were soon dispersed; that some of the police fired on the men while they were running and wounded a large number who were already 100 feet or more away and were running as fast as they could; that at least four of the number so shot down died; that this was wanton and unprovoked murder, but there was not even so much as an investigation.

WAS IT AN ACT OF PERSONAL REVENGE?

While some men may tamely submit to being clubbed and seeing their brothers shot down, there are some who will resent it, and will nurture a spirit of hatred and seek revenge for themselves, and the occurrences that preceded the Haymarket tragedy indicate that the bomb was thrown by someone who, instead of acting on the advice of anybody, was simply seeking personal revenge for having been clubbed, and that Capt. Bonfield is the man who is really responsible for the death of the police officers.

It is also shown that the character of the Haymarket meeting sustains this view. The evidence shows that there were only 800 to 1,000 people present, and that it was a peaceable and orderly meeting; that the mayor of the city was present and saw nothing out of the way, and that he remained until the crowd began to disperse, the meeting being practically over, and the crowd engaged in dispersing when he left; that had the police remained away for twenty minutes more there would have been nobody left there, but as soon as Bonfield had learned that the mayor had left, he could not resist the temptation to have some more people clubbed, and went up with a detachment of police to disperse the meeting; and that on the appearance of the police the bomb was thrown by some unknown person, and several innocent and faithful officers, who were simply obeying an uncalled-for order of their superior, were killed. All of these facts tend to show the improbability of the theory of the prosecution that the bomb was thrown as a result of a conspiracy on the part of the defendants to commit murder; if the theory of the prosecution were correct, there would have been many more bombs thrown; and the fact that only one was thrown shows that it was an act of personal revenge.

It is further shown here, that much of the evidence given at the trial was a pure fabrication; that some of the prominent police officials, in their zeal, not only terrorized ignorant men by throwing them into prison and threatening them with torture if they refused to swear to anything desired, but that they offered money and employment to those who would consent to do this. Further, that they deliberately planned to have fictitious conspiracies formed in order that they might get the glory of discovering them. In addition to the evidence in the record of some witnesses who swore that they had been paid small sums of money, etc., several documents are here referred to.

First, an interview with Capt. Ebersold, published in the Chicago Daily News, May 10, 1889.

CHIEF OF POLICE EBERSOLD'S STATEMENT

Ebersold was chief of police of Chicago at the time of the Haymarket trouble, and for a long time before and thereafter, so that he was in a position to know what was going on, and his utterances upon this point are therefore important. Among other things he says:

"It was my policy to quiet matters down as soon as possible after the 4th of May. The general unsettled state of things was an injury to Chicago.

"On the other hand, Capt. Schaack wanted to keep things stirring. He wanted bombs to be found here, there, all around, everywhere. I thought people would lie down and sleep better if they were not afraid that their homes would be blown to pieces any minute. But this man Schaack, this little boy who must have glory or his heart would be broken, wanted none of that policy. Now, here is something the public does not know. After we got the anarchist societies broken up, Schaack wanted to send out men to again organize new societies right away. You see what this would do. He wanted to keep the thing boiling—keep himself prominent before the public. Well, I sat down on that; I didn't believe in such work, and of course Schaack didn't like it.

"After I heard all that, I began to think there was, perhaps, not so much to all this anarchist business as they claimed, and I believe I was right. Schaack thinks he knew all about those anarchists. Why, I knew more at that time than he knows to-day about them. I was following them closely. As soon as Schaack began to get some notoriety, however, he was spoiled."

This is a most important statement, when a chief of police, who has been watching the anarchists closely, says that he was convinced that there was not so much in all their anarchist business as was claimed, and that a police captain wanted to send out men to have other conspiracies formed, in order to get the credit of discovering them, and keep the public excited; it throws a flood of light on the whole situation and destroys the force of much of the testimony introduced at the trial.

For, if there has been any such extensive conspiracy as the prosecution claims, the police would have soon discovered it. No chief of police could discover a determination on the part of an individual, or even a number of separate individuals, to have personal revenge for having been maltreated, nor could any chief discover a determination by any such individual to kill the next policeman who might assault him. Consequently, the fact that the police did not discover any conspiracy before the Haymarket affair, shows almost conclusively that no such extensive combination could have existed.

As further bearing on the question of creating evidence, reference is made to the following affidavits:

STATE OF ILLINOIS, ⎱ ss.
    County of Cook. ⎰

Jacob Mikolanda, being first duly sworn, on oath, states that he took no part in the so-called May troubles of 1886; that on or about the 8th day of May, 1886, two police officers without a warrant, or without assigning any reason therefor, took this affiant from a saloon, where he was conducting himself peacefully, and obliged him to accompany them to his house; that the same officers entered his house without a search warrant, and ransacked the same, not even permitting the baby's crib, with its sleeping occupant, to escape their unlawful and fruitless search; that about a month after this occurrence, this affiant was summoned by Officer Peceny to accompany him to the police station, as Lieutenant Shepard wished to speak to me; that there, without a warrant, affiant was thrown into jail; that he was thereupon shown some photographs and asked if he knew the persons, and on answering to the affirmative as to some of the pictures, he was again thrown into prison; that he was then transferred from one station to another for several days; that he was importuned by a police captain and Assistant State's Attorney to turn State's witness, being promised therefor money, the good will and protection of the police, their political influence in securing a position and his entire freedom; and on answering that he knew nothing to which he could testify, he was thrown back into jail; that his preliminary hearing was repeatedly continued for want of prosecution, each continuance obliging this affiant to remain longer in jail; that eventually this affiant was dismissed for want of prosecution.

JACOB MIKOLANDA.

Subscribed and sworn to before me this 14th day of April, A.D. 1893.

CHARLES B. PAVLICEK,
Notary Public.

STATE OF ILLINOIS, ⎱ ss.
    County of Cook. ⎰

Vaclav Djmek, being first duly sworn, on oath states that he knows of no cause for his arrest on the 7th day of May, A.D. 1886; that he took no part in any of the troubles of the preceding days; that without a warrant for his arrest, or without a search warrant for his premises, the police entered the house on the night of the 7th of May, 1886; that on being requested to show by what authority they entered, the police heaped abuse upon this affiant and his wife; that the police then proceeded to ransack the house, roused this affiant's little children out of bed, pulled the same to pieces, carried away the affiant's papers and pillow slips, because the same were red; that on the way to the police station, though this affiant offered no resistance whatever, and went at the command of the officer, peacefully, this affiant was choked, covered by revolvers, and otherwise inhumanly treated by the police officers; that for many days this affiant was jailed and refused a preliminary hearing; that during said time he was threatened, and promised immunity by the police, if he would turn State's witness; that the police clerk and officer Johnson repeatedly promised this affiant his freedom and considerable money, if he would turn State's witness; that on his protestations that he knew nothing to which he could testify, this affiant was abused and ill-treated; that while he was jailed this affiant was kicked, clubbed, beaten and scratched, had curses and abuses heaped upon him, and was threatened with hanging by the police; that this affiant's wife was abused by the police when she sought permission to see this affiant.

VACLAV DJMEK.

Subscribed and sworn to before me, this 14th day of April, A.D. 1893.

CHARLES B. PAVLICEK,
Notary Public.

I will simply say in conclusion, on this branch of the case, that the facts tend to show that the bomb was thrown as an act of personal revenge, and that the prosecution has never discovered who threw it, and the evidence utterly fails to show that the man who did throw it ever heard or read a word coming from the defendants; consequently it fails to show that he acted on any advice given by them. And if he did not act on or hear any advice coming from the defendants, either in speeches or through the press, then there was no case against them, even under the law as laid down by Judge Gary.

FIELDEN AND SCHWAB

At the trial a number of detectives and members of the police swore that the defendant, Fielden at the Haymarket meeting, made threat to kill, urging his hearers to do their duty as he would do his, just as the policemen were coming up; and one policeman swears that Fielden drew a revolver and fired at the police while he was standing on the wagon before the bomb was thrown, while some of the others testified that he first climbed down off the wagon and fired while standing by a wheel. On the other hand, it was proven by a number of witnesses, and by facts and circumstances, that this evidence must be absolutely untrue. A number of newspaper reporters, who testified on the part of the State, said that they were standing near Fielden—

much nearer than the police were—and heard all that was said and saw what was done; that they had been sent there for that purpose, and that Fielden did not make any such threats as the police swore to, and that he did not use a revolver. A number of other men who were near, too, and some of them on the wagon on which Fielden stood at the time, swear to the same thing. Fielden himself swears that he did not make any such threats as the police swore to, and further, that he never had or used a revolver in his life. But if there were any doubt about the fact that the evidence charging Fielden with having used a revolver as unworthy of credit, it is removed by Judge Gary and State's Attorney Grinnell. On November 8, 1887, when the question of commuting the death sentence as to Fielden was before the Governor, Judge Gary wrote a long letter in regard to the case in which, in speaking of Fielden, he, among other things, says: "There is in the nature and private character of the man a love of justice, an impatience at undeserved sufferings. . . . In his own private life he was the honest, industrious and peaceful laboring man. In what he said in court before sentence he was respectful and decorous. His language and conduct since have been irreproachable. As there is no evidence that he knew of any preparation to do the specific act of throwing the bomb that killed Degan, he does not understand even now that general advice to large masses to do violence makes him responsible for the violence done by reason of that advice. . . . In short, he was more a misguided enthusiast than a criminal conscious of the horrible nature and effect of his teachings and of his responsibility therefor."

The State's Attorney appended the foregoing letter, beginning as follows: "While endorsing and approving the foregoing statement by Judge Gary, I wish to add thereto the suggestion . . . that Schwab's conduct during the trial, and when addressing the court before sentence, like Fielden's, was decorous, respectful to the law and commendable. . . . It is further my desire to say that I believe that Schwab was the pliant, weak tool of a stronger will and more designing person. Schwab seems to be friendless."

If what Judge Gary says about Fielden is true; if Fielden has "a natural love of justice and in his private life was the honest,

industrious and peaceable laboring man," then Fielden's testimony is entitled to credit, and when he says that he did not
do the things the police charge him with doing, and that he
never had or used a revolver in his life, it is probably true, especially as he is corroborated by a number of creditable and dis-
interested witnesses.

Again, if Fielden did the things the police charged him with
doing, if he fired on them as they swear, then he was not a mere
misguided enthusiast, who was to be held only for the consequences of his teachings; and if either Judge Gary or State's
Attorney Grinnell had placed any reliance on the evidence of
the police on this point, they would have written a different
kind of letter to the then executive.

In the fall of 1887, a number of the most prominent business
men of Chicago met to consult whether or not to ask for executive clemency for any of the condemned men. Mr. Grinnell was
present and made a speech, in which, in referring to this evidence, he said that he had serious doubts whether Fielden had
a revolver on that occasion, or whether indeed Fielden ever
had one.

Yet, in arguing the case before the Supreme Court the previous spring, much stress was placed by the State on the evidence relating to what Fielden did at the Haymarket meeting,
and that court was misled into attaching great importance to it.

It is now clear that there is no case made out against Fielden
for anything he did on that night, and, as heretofore shown, in
order to hold him and the other defendants for the consequences
and effects of having given pernicious and criminal advice to
large masses to commit violence, whether orally, in speeches, or
in print, it must be shown that the person committing the violence had read or heard the advice; for, until he had heard or
read it, he did not receive, and if he never received the advice,
it cannot be said that he acted on it.

STATE'S ATTORNEY ON NEEBE'S INNOCENCE

IV. At the conclusion of the evidence for the State, the Hon.
Carter H. Harrison, then Mayor of Chicago, and Mr. F. S. Winston, then Corporation Counsel for Chicago, were in the court
room and had a conversation with Mr. Grinnell, the State's At-

torney, in regard to the evidence against Neebe, in which conversation, according to Mr. Harrison and Mr. Winston, the State's Attorney said that he did not think he had a case against Neebe, and that he wanted to dismiss him, but was dissuaded from doing so by his associate attorneys, who feared that such a step might influence the jury in favor of the other defendants.

Mr. Harrison, in a letter, among other things, says: "I was present in the court room when the State closed its case. The attorney for Neebe moved his discharge on the ground that there was no evidence to hold him on. The State's Attorney, Mr. Julius S. Grinnell, and Mr. Fred S. Winston, Corporation Counsel for the city, and myself, were in earnest conversation when the motion was made. Mr. Grinnell stated to us that he did not think there was sufficient testimony to convict Neebe. I thereupon earnestly advised him, as the representative of the State, to dismiss the case as to Neebe, and, if I remember rightly, he was seriously thinking of doing so, but, on consultation with his assistants, and on their advice, he determined not to do so, lest it would have an injurious effect on the case as against the other prisoners. . . . I took the position that such discharge, being clearly justified by the testimony, would not prejudice the case as to the others."

Mr. Winston adds the following to Mr. Harrison's letter:

March 21, 1889.

I concur in the statement of Mr. Harrison; I never believed there was sufficient evidence to convict Mr. Neebe, and so stated during the trial.

F. S. WINSTON.

In January, 1890, Mr. Grinnell wrote a letter to Gov. Fifer, denying that he had ever made any such statement as that mentioned by Mr. Harrison and Mr. Winston; also that he did believe Neebe guilty; that Mr. Harrison suggested the dismissal of the case as to Neebe; and further, that he would not have been surprised if Mr. Harrison had made a similar suggestion as to others, and then he says: "I said to Mr. Harrison at that time, substantially, that I was afraid that the jury might not think the testimony presented in the case sufficient to convict Neebe, but that it was in their province to pass upon it."

Now, if the statement of Messrs. Harrison and Winston is

true, then Grinnell should not have allowed Neebe to be sent to the penitentiary, and even if we assume that both Mr. Harrison and Mr. Winston are mistaken, and that Mr. Grinnell simply used the language he now says he used, then the case must have seemed very weak to him. If, with a jury prejudiced to start with, a judge pressing for conviction, and amid the almost irresistible fury with which the trial was conducted, he still was afraid the jury might not think the testimony in the case was sufficient to convict Neebe, then the testimony must have seemed very weak to him, no matter what he may now protest about it.

When the motion to dismiss the case as to Neebe was made, defendants' counsel asked that the jury might be permitted to retire while the motion was being argued, but the court refused to permit this, and kept the jury present where it could hear all that the court had to say; then when the argument on the motion was begun by defendants' counsel, the court did not wait to hear from the attorneys for the State, but at once proceeded to argue the points itself with the attorneys for the defendants, so that while the attorneys for the State made no argument on the motion, twenty-five pages of the record are filled with the colloquy or sparring that took place between the court and the counsel for the defendants, the court in the presence of the jury making insinuations as to what inference might be drawn by the jury from the fact that Neebe owned a little stock in a paper called the Arbeiter Zeitung and had been seen there, although he took no part in the management until after the Haymarket troubles, it appearing that the Arbeiter Zeitung had published some very seditious articles, with which, however, Neebe had nothing to do. Finally one of the counsel for the defendants said: "I expected that the representatives of the State might say something, but as your honor saves them that trouble, you will excuse me if I reply briefly to the suggestions you have made." Some other remarks were made by the court, seriously affecting the whole case and prejudicial to the defendants, and then, referring to Neebe, the court said:

"Whether he had anything to do with the dissemination of advice to commit murder is, I think, a debatable question which the jury ought to pass on." Finally the motion was overruled.

Now, with all the eagerness shown by the court to convict Neebe, it must have regarded the evidence against him as very weak, otherwise it would not have made this admission, for if it was a debatable question whether the evidence tended to show guilt, then that evidence must have been far from being conclusive upon the question as to whether he was actually guilty; this being so, the verdict should not have been allowed to stand, because the law requires that a man shall be proven to be guilty beyond a reasonable doubt before he can be convicted of criminal offense. I have examined all of the evidence against Neebe with care, and it utterly fails to prove even the shadow of a case against him. Some of the other defendants were guilty of using seditious language, but even this cannot be said of Neebe.

PREJUDICE OR SUBSERVIENCY OF JUDGE

V. It is further charged, with much bitterness, by those who speak for the prisoners, that the record of this case shows that the judge conducted the trial with malicious ferocity, and forced eight men to be tried together; that in cross-examining the State's witnesses, he confined counsel to the specific points touched on by the State, while in the cross-examination of the defendants' witnesses he permitted the State's Attorney to go into all manner of subjects entirely foreign to the matters on which the witnesses were examined in chief; also, that every ruling throughout the long trial on any contested point, was in favor of the State; and further, that page after page of the record contains insinuating remarks of the judge, made in the hearing of the jury, and with the evident intent of bringing the jury to his way of thinking; that these speeches, coming from the court, were much more damaging than any speeches from the State's Attorney could possibly have been; that the State's Attorney often took his cue from the judge's remarks; that the judge's magazine article recently published, although written nearly six years after the trial, is yet full of venom; that, pretending to simply review the case, he had to drag into his article a letter written by an excited woman to a newspaper after the trial was over, and which therefore had nothing to do with the case, and was put into the articles simply to create a prejudice against the woman, as well as against the dead and the living; and that, not content with this, he, in the same article, makes an insinuating attack on one of the lawyers for the defense, not for anything done at the trial, but because more than a year after the trial, when some of the defendants had been hung, he ventured to express a few kind, if erroneous, sentiments over the graves of his dead clients, whom he at least believed to be innocent. It is urged that such ferocity of subserviency is without a parallel in all history; that even Jeffries in England, contented himself with hanging his victims, and did not stoop to berate them after death.

These charges are of a personal character, and while they seem to be sustained by the record of the trial and the papers before me, and tend to show the trial was not fair, I do not care to discuss this feature of the case any farther, because it is not necessary. I am convinced that it is clearly my duty to act in this case for the reasons already given, and I, therefore, grant an absolute pardon to Samuel Fielden, Oscar Neebe and Michael Schwab, this 26th day of June, 1893.

JOHN P. ALTGELD,
Governor of Illinois.

"ADDRESS TO THE LABORING MEN OF CHICAGO"

Delivered at Chicago, September 8, 1893

As reformer, as judge, and as Governor of Illinois, John Peter Altgeld
was a friend and champion of laboring men and their families. But
he did not hesitate to speak realistically and even bluntly in assessing
the position of labor. In this address he painted a grim and depress-
ing picture of the years immediately ahead, and called for a strength-
ening of the trade union movement.

You are to be congratulated on the success of your celebra-
tion. Two great demonstrations in Chicago alone are vying with
each other in honoring Labor Day. These vast assemblages represent sturdy manhood and womanhood. They represent honest
toil of every kind, and they represent strong patriotism and
desirable citizenship. The law has set apart this day in recognition of the nobility of labor, and as the Governor of this great
State, I have come to pay homage to that force which lays the
foundation of empires, which builds cities, builds railroads,
develops agriculture, supports schools, founds industries, creates
commerce, and moves the world. It is wisely directed labor that
has made our country the greatest ever known, and has made
Chicago the wonder of mankind. I say wisely directed labor;
for without wise direction labor is fruitless. The pointing out and
the doing are inseparably connected. More than this, ahead of
the directing, there must go the genius which originates and con-
ceives, the genius which takes the risk and moves a league

forward. All three are necessary to each other. Weaken either, and there are clouds in the sky. Destroy either, and the hammer of industry ceases to be heard. Glance over this majestic city, see its workshops, its warehouses, its commercial palaces, its office temples, and the thousand other structures that show the possibilities of human achievement and tell who did all this. You say the laboring men; yes, that is correct; but I tell you that if the gods keep a record of our doings, they have set down the men who originated all this, and then dared to make a forward step in building, as among the greatest of laborers. We are at present in the midst of a great industrial and commercial depression. Industry is nearly at a stand-still all over the earth. The consumptive power, or rather the purchasing power, of the world has been interfered with, producing not only a derangement but a paralysis, not only stopping further production, but preventing the proper distribution of what there is already created; so that we have the anomalous spectacle of abundant food products on the one hand, and hungry men without bread on the other. Abundant fabrics on the one hand, and industrious, frugal men going half clad on the other. Employer and employe are affected alike.

There are thousands of honest, industrious and frugal men who walk the streets all day in search of work, and even bread, and there are many hundreds of the most enterprising employers who sweat by day and walk the floor by night trying to devise means to keep the sheriff away from the establishment. You are not responsible for this condition. Men here and in Europe, who call themselves statesmen, have inaugurated policies of which this is a natural result. Considering the increase in population, the increase in the industries and commercial activity of the world, as well as the increased area over which business was done, there has in recent years been a practical reduction in the volume of the money of the world of from thirty-three to forty per cent., and there had of necessity to follow a shrinkage in the value of property to a corresponding extent. This has been going on for a number of years, and as it has progressed it has become harder and harder for the debtor to meet his obligations. For the value of his property kept falling while his debt did not fall. Consequently, every little while a lot of debtors, who could no longer stand the strain, succumbed. The result was that each time there was a flurry in financial circles. By degrees these failures became more frequent, until finally people who had money took alarm, and withdrew it from circulation. This precipitated a panic and with it a harvest of bankruptcy. No doubt there were secondary causes that contributed, but this one cause was sufficient to create the distress that we see. If for some years to come there should not be sufficient blood in the industrial and commercial world to make affairs healthy, then you must console yourselves with the thought that our country, with all the other great nations, has been placed on a narrow gold basis, and you will not be troubled with any of these cheap dollars that the big newspapers claim you did not want. The present depression, resulting from a lack of ready money in the world, shows how indispensable capital is to labor—all the wheels of industry stand still the moment it is withdrawn. It also shows that while the interests of the employer and the employe may be antagonistic on the subject of wages, they are the same in every other respect; neither can do anything without the other—certain it is that the employe cannot prosper unless the employer does. On the other hand, if the purchasing power of the employe is destroyed, the employer must soon be without a market for his goods. The great American market was due to the purchasing power of the laboring classes. If this should in the end be destroyed it will change entirely the character of our institutions. Whenever our laboring classes are reduced to a condition where they can buy only a few coarse articles of food and clothing, then our glory will have departed. Still another thing has been made more clear than before, and that is, that the employers, as a rule, are not great capitalists of the country. As a rule, they are enterprising men who borrow idle capital, and put it to some use, and whenever they are suddenly called on to pay up and are not able to borrow elsewhere, they are obliged to shut down.

There are many advanced thinkers who look forward to a new industrial system that shall be an improvement on the present, and under which the laborer shall come nearer getting his share of the benefits resulting from invention and machinery, than under the present system. All lovers of their kind would hail such a system with joy. But we are forced to say that it is not yet at hand. As we must have bread and must have clothing, we are obliged to cling to the old system for the present, and probably for a long time to come, until the foundations can be laid for a better one by intelligent progress. Classes, like individuals, have their bright and their dark days, and just now there seems to be a long dark day ahead of you. It will be a day of suffering and distress, and I must say to you there seems to be no way of escaping it, and I therefore counsel you to face it squarely and bear it with that heroism and fortitude with which an American citizen should face and bear calamity. It has been suggested that the State and different branches of government should furnish employment during the winter to idle men. Certainly everything that can be done in this line will be done, but I must warn you not to expect too much from this source. The powers of government are so hedged about with constitutional provisions that much cannot be done. The State at present has no work to do. The parks can employ only a few men. The city has work for more men, but it is also limited in its funds. The great drainage canal may, and probably will, give employment to a considerable number of men, but, after all, you must recognize that these things will be only in the nature of makeshifts; only to tide over; only to keep men and their families from starving. And on this point let me say it will be the duty of all public officials to see to it that no man is permitted to starve on the soil of Illinois, and provision will be made to that end. But all this is temporary. The laborer must look to ways and means that are permanent for the improvement of his condition when the panic is over, and these measures must be along the line of and in harmony with the institutions of this century, and must move by a gradual and steady development. Nothing that is violently done is of permanent advantage to the working man. He can only prosper when his labor is in demand, and his labor can be in demand only when his employer prospers and there is nothing to interfere with consumption.

The world has been slow to accord labor its due. For thousands of years pillage, plunder and organized robbery, called warfare, were honorable pursuits, and the man who toiled, in order that all might live, was despised. In the flight of time, it was but yesterday that the labor of the earth was driven with the lash, and either sold on the block like cattle, or tied by an invisible chain to the soil, and was forbidden to even wander outside his parish. In the yesterday of time, even the employers of labor were despised. The men who conducted great industries, who carried on commerce, who practiced the useful arts, the men who made the earth habitable, were looked down upon by a class than considered it honorable to rob the toiler of his bread, a class which, while possessing the pride of the eagle, had only the character of the vulture. Great has been the development since then. This century brought upon its wings higher ideas, more of truth and more of common sense, and it announced to mankind that he is honorable who creates; that he should be despised who can only consume; that he is the benefactor of the race who gives it an additional thought, an additional flower, an additional loaf of bread, an additional comfort; and he is a curse to his kind who tramples down what others build, or, without compensation, devours what others create. The century brought with it still greater things. Not only did it lift the employer to a position of honor, influence and power, but it tore away parish boundaries, it cut the chains of the serf, it burned the auction block, where the laborer and his children were sold; and it brought ideas; it taught the laboring man to extend his hand to his fellow-laborer; it taught him to organize, and not only to read but to investigate, to inquire, to discuss, to consider and to look ahead; so that to-day, the laborer and his cause, at least theoretically, command the homage of all civilized men, and the greatest States in christendom have set apart a day to be annually observed as a holiday in honor of labor.

The children of Israel were forty years in marching from the bondage of Egypt to the freer atmosphere of Palestine, and a halo of glory envelops their history. In the last forty years the children of Toil have made a forward march which is greater than any ever made in the wilderness. True, the land is not conquered. You have simply camped upon that higher plane where you can more clearly see the difficulties of the past, and where, in the end, you may hope for a higher justice and a happier condition for yourselves and your children, but a great deal remains to be done. In a sense, you are just out of the wilderness. You ask, along what lines, then, shall we proceed when the times get better in order to improve our condition? I answer, along lines which harmonize, not only with nature's laws, but with the laws of the land. Occupying, as I do, a position which makes me in a sense a conservator of all interests and classes, I desire to see the harmonious prosperity of all; and let me say to you that, until all the active interests of the land prosper again, there can be no general demand for your services, and consequently, no healthy prosperity. What I wish to point out is the absolute necessity of each class or interest being able to take care of itself in the fierce struggle for existence. You have not yet fully reached this state. In the industrial world, as well as in the political world, only those forces survive which can maintain themselves, and which are so concentrated that their influence is immediately and directly felt. A scattered force, no matter how great, is of no account in the sharp contests of the age. This is an age of concentration. Everywhere there is concentration and combination of capital and of those factors which to-day rule the world. The formation of corporations has greatly accelerated this movement, and no matter what is said about it, whether we approve it or not, it is the characteristic feature of our civilization, and grows out of increased invention, the speedy communication between different parts of the world, and the great industrial generalship and enterprise of the time. It is questionable whether this tendency to combination could have been stopped in any way. It is certain, without this concentration of force, the gigantic achievements of our times would have been an impossibility. Combination and concentration are the masters of the age. Let the laborer learn from this and act accordingly. Fault-finding and idle complaint are useless. Great forces, like great rivers, cannot be stopped. You must be able to fight your own battles. For the laborer to stand single-handed before giant combinations of power means annihilation. The world gives only when it is obliged to, and respects only those who compel its respect.

Government was created by power and has always been controlled by power. Do not imagine that it is sufficient if you have justice and equity on your side, for the earth is covered with the graves of justice and equity that failed to receive recognition,

because there was no influence or force to compel it, and it will
be so until the millennium. Whenever you demonstrate that you
are an active, concentrated power, moving along lawful lines,
then you will be felt in government. Until then you will not.
This is an age of law as well as of force, and no force succeeds
that does not move along legal lines. The laboring men of the
world always have been, and are to-day, the support and principal reliance of the government. They support its flags in time
of war, and their hands earn the taxes in time of peace. Their
voice is for fair play, and no great government was ever destroyed by the laboring classes. Treason and rebellion never originated with them, but always came from the opposite source.
Early in our history there occurred what was called Shay's
rebellion, but they were not wage-workers who created it. Then
came the so-called whisky rebellion, created not by day laborers.
During the war of 1812, a convention was held in the East
which practically advocated a dissolution of the Union, but
wage-workers were not among its members. The great rebellion
of 1861 was not fomented by the laboring classes, but by those
classes which ate the bread that others toiled for. It was a rebellion by those who had long been prominent as leaders, who
largely controlled the wealth of the country, who boasted of
aristocratic society, and many of whom had been educated at the
expense of the country whose flag they fired on. While, on the
other hand, the great armies which put down this rebellion and
supported the flag were composed of men who had literally
earned their bread by the sweat of their brows. It is true that
at times a number of laborers, more or less ignorant, who thought
they were being robbed of the fruits of their toil, have indulged
in rioting; and, while they have always lost by it, and while
they cannot be too severely condemned, yet they do not stand
alone in this condemnation, for there have been many broadcloth mobs in this country and in different sections of it, whose
actions were lawless and as disgraceful as that of any labor mob
that ever assembled. I must congratulate organized labor upon
its freedom from turbulence. Rioting is nearly always by an
ignorant class outside of all organizations, and which, in most
cases, was brought into the community by conscienceless men to
defeat organized labor. There should be a law compelling a man

who brings this class of people into our midst to give bond for their support and their good behavior, for at present they are simply a disturbing element. They threaten the peace of society and bring reproach on the cause of labor. The lesson I wish to impress upon you is that in business, in the industries, in government, everywhere, only those interests and forces survive that can maintain themselves along legal lines, and if you permanently improve your condition it must be by intelligently and patriotically standing together all over the country. Every plan must fail unless you do this.

At present you are to a great extent yet a scattered force, sufficiently powerful, if collected, to make yourselves heard and felt; to secure, not only a fair hearing, but a fair decision of all questions. Unite this power and you will be independent; leave it scattered and you will fail. Organization is the result of education as well as an educator. Let all the men of America who toil with their hands once stand together and no more complaints will be heard about unfair treatment. The progress of labor in the future must be along the line of patriotic association, not simply in localities, but everywhere. And let me caution you that every act of violence is a hindrance to your progress. There will be men among you ready to commit it. They are your enemies. There will be sneaks and Judas Iscariots in your ranks, who will for a mere pittance act as spies and try to incite some of the more hot-headed of your number to deeds of violence, in order that these reptiles may get the credit of exposing you. They are your enemies. Cast them out of your ranks. Remember that any permanent prosperity must be based upon intelligence and upon conditions which are permanent. And let me say to you again, in conclusion: This fall and this winter will be a trying time to you. The record of the laborers of the earth is one of patriotism. They have maintained the government, they have maintained the schools and churches, and it behooves you now to face the hardships that are upon you and see that your cause is not injured by grave indiscretions. Make the ignorant understand that government is strong and that life and property will be protected and law and order will be maintained, and that, while the day is dark now, the future will place the laborer in a more exalted position than he has ever occupied.

ADDRESS COMMEMORATING INSTALLATION OF THE NEW PRESIDENT OF THE UNIVERSITY OF ILLINOIS

Delivered at Champaign, May, 1895

Of all the causes and institutions which engaged the attention and sympathy of Governor Altgeld, none was closer to his heart than the University of Illinois and its growing role in both state and national perspectives. At every opportunity, he strongly supported the University and its goals. In this address he outlines his hopes for the University.

The growth of an educational institution is like that of a man and cannot be accomplished in a day or in a year. There must be a period of infancy, of childhood and of boyhood before the vigor of manhood is reached. So with an institution of learning. There is the weak beginning, the early struggle, the later growth, and then the fullgrown university, and as the ultimate greatness of the man is often in proportion to his early struggles, so the final career and usefulness of an institution is frequently determined by the difficulties it surmounts in its infancy. A college or university is not simply a machine. It is not negative, but positive in character. It does more than teach algebra and Latin. It has an independent existence and makes its impression on all who come in contact with it. Its character is a force that creeps silently over the land, and by day and by night molds the sentiments of men. It is this character by which an institution is judged. The world does not care so much for the number of students but it asks what is the character of the institution? What does it stand for? Does it stand for a sturdy, stalwart, patriotic manhood, and the earnest, serious, hard work that goes with it? If yea, then great will be its influence. But if it represents only the easy-going standards of mediocrity or a dudish dilettanteism, then it will not shape the destinies of the nation. There have been colleges that were small and financially poor and were attended mostly by the sons of the poor, but they gave to their country whole constellations of great men, while others that were both large and rich did little more than furnish amusement for inherited wealth. The University of Illinois has passed through the stages of infancy and youth, and has arrived at a point where it should embark on a career of fullgrown and vigorous manhood. Much conscientious work has been done. The men who builded it toiled hard and laid the foundations broad and deep, and I believe that the structure which has been reared on these foundations is an enduring one, but we must broaden its influence and enlarge its work; we must bring it to the attention of our people. Few of them know of its great advantages. Few of them know that the agricultural experiment station does not constitute all that there is, but is only incidental and gives so much of an additional advantage. Few of them know that the students, without extra expense and without loss of time, have the advantage of being trained in the military art by a United States military officer. And very few of them know that we have here one of the best equipped engineering schools, particularly in the department of electrical engineering, that there is in the whole country.

As the executive of the State I feel a deep interest in all of its institutions, and I feel an especial interest in this university. The State of Illinois leads all others in point of material grandeur, in point of natural wealth. It leads all others in the energy and enterprise of its people, and it leads all others in having a most romantic and wonderful history. Illinois already stands foremost among the great States of the earth. The achievements of its people have already won the admiration of the civilized world, and we must have an educational institution that will be on the same plane of greatness and of the same high character. We have over this State numerous colleges and seminaries that are doing excellent work and we should have here a university which could offer to the graduates of those institutions higher advantages. We should have here all of the machinery, the instruments, the models, and the specimens that are necessary in modern education. I am anxious to have a university here to which our people can send their young men and their young women, instead of sending them East; a university that shall perpetuate the rugged strength and stalwart manhood which characterizes the people of the Mississippi Valley. We want an institution which shall be free from the dilettanteism that is weakening the East, and that shall inculcate those fundamental principles of liberty, of national union and supremacy, and of local self-government that have given our country its marvelous career of progress and development. We want an institution that shall be thoroughly modern in spirit and effort, and from whose halls shall go forth men and women of such strong moral fiber, such industry and such fervor of soul, that they will lead our people on to loftier planes and to greater glory. We must have in this State a university that will hold aloft the flame of American civilization so that all the people in the world may be blessed by its light. We must have a university whose fame shall be co-extensive with civilization.

I trust that this occasion may prove to be more than merely an entertainment, more than a passing event that leaves only a pleasant recollection. I trust that there may go forth from this meeting a spirit that will arouse all of our people, and that all of us who are in any way connected with this institution may have renewed inspiration and may go forth with higher and nobler resolves in our efforts to make this university represent the great common people of this country; make it the friend and the helper of the toiling masses, of those people who do the work of the world, the people who lay the foundation of empires, who subdue rebellions, who fight for liberty, who build cities, railroads, churches and schools, the people who make our civilization.

We have met to install a new chief. I have told you what we

want to make of this institution. We needed a man to put in charge of this work who was more than a scholar, more than an educator, more even than a general; a man who, while possessing all of these qualifications, was also thoroughly imbued with the spirit of the age, with a sense of the needs of our people; a man who was not only progressive, but aggressive. We believe we have found that man.

ADDRESS ON THE GOLD STANDARD, BEFORE THE DEMOCRATIC NATIONAL CONVENTION OF 1896

Delivered at Chicago, July 8, 1896

Determined that the Democratic party should espouse a consistently progressive outlook, Altgeld threw his energies to that end in the 1896 Democratic National Convention. He was not overly fond of William Jennings Bryan, but felt him to be the best progressive candidate available. Altgeld's influence was considered decisive in the naming of Bryan as the Democratic presidential nominee in 1896, and it is thought that if Altgeld had not been disqualified for the Presidency because of place of birth, he himself might have been selected as nominee. In any case, Altgeld's philosophy was reflected in every aspect of the 1896 Democratic platform, and he had convincingly demonstrated his power and stature as a national political figure.

This address presents Altgeld's outlook on the merits of free silver as opposed to the gold standard, a key question considered by the convention and resolved in accordance with Altgeld's viewpoint.

I did not come here to make speeches. I came here to assist in nominating the next President of these United States. I came here to assist in formulating a declaration of principles that shall again offer hope to our people.

Rarely in the history of government has an assembly of free men been confronted with such far-reaching questions—with questions that are fraught with so much of weal or woe to human kind—as those with which this convention must deal. For a number of years there has existed in Europe and in our country stagnation in trade, paralysis of industry and a suspension of enterprise. We have seen the streets of our cities filled with idle men, with hungry women and with ragged children. The country to-day looks to the deliberations of this convention for promise of relief.

In order to deal intelligently with these unhappy conditions, it is necessary to glance for a moment at the cause which produced them. During the decade which followed the civil war we became the great debtor people of the earth. Everything from the government down to the sewing machine of the seamstress was mortgaged. There were the great national, State, city, county and other municipal debts. There were the great railroad and other corporation debts. There were the farm and city mortgages, the great private indebtedness, all amounting to thousands of millions of dollars and nearly all held by English money lenders.

The interest on this great indebtedness had to be paid every year out of the toil of our people, but under the conditions as they then existed, we met those payments and our people had a surplus. They were able, in addition, to supply themselves with the necessities and comforts and even the luxuries of life. As a consequence the farmer prospered, the manufacturer prospered and labor was employed. But, unhappily for the world, the large security-holding classes conceived the idea that it would be to their interest to make money dear and property and labor cheap.

It being an immutable law of finance that when you increase the volume of money in the world you increase the selling price of property and things, so, on the other hand, when you reduce the volume of money in the world you reduce the selling price of property and labor.

These gentlemen determined to destroy one-half of the money of the world, and between 1873 and 1880 they got our government and the governments of Europe to arbitrarily, by law, strike down silver. They demonetized it; they stopped its coinage; they took away its legal tender functions; they reduced it to the position of token money, where it was used at all. The effect of this was to double the burden that was put upon gold.

Formerly the two metals together did the work of the business world. After that time the one metal alone had to do all the business of the world. Consequently the number of people who had to have it were doubled. It was doubled in importance and its purchasing power was doubled so that thereafter the gold dollar bought twice as much labor, twice as much property, twice as much of the bread and sweat of mankind as it did before.

Not only this, but they reduced by one-half the annual addition to the stock of money of the world. Formerly there was added every year all of the silver and all of the gold produced to the world's stock of primary or redemption money. Since that time there is added every year only the gold produced, so that we have a constantly shrinking standard of value with a constantly increasing population, which means a constantly decreasing scale of prices.

When these great debts were created, the world's standard and the world's measure of values consisted of the sum total of the two metals considered practically as one. They formed the standard of prices. To-day the standard of prices consists of only one metal, and it is only half as high as it was when it consisted of the two, and, as a consequence prices to-day are only half as high as they were when we had the two metals.

What has been the result? Why, to-day it takes all that the farmer, all that the producer can scrape together to pay these fixed charges; all that he can get to pay interest, taxes and other fixed charges; for, mind you, this great debt was not reduced, interest was not reduced, taxes were not reduced. On the contrary, they were higher than they were, and as a result our American market has been destroyed. The farmer now can not buy as much at the store as he formerly could. The farmer is prostrated, the merchant does less business, the railroads do less business, the manufacturer can not sell his product and the laborer finds that there is nobody to buy the things that he makes, therefore he is out of employment. Physicians tell us that if you take half of the blood out of the human body the remainder congests at the heart and the extremities grow cold and lifeless. That is what happened in this case. With abundant harvests the world is in distress. Now, the question is, shall we continue this system or shall we restore the former standard?

Gentlemen, we are offering nothing new. We are suggesting

no experiments. We are simply declaring that when you pay a creditor in the same kind of money which he gave you, you are doing everything that God or man can ask at your hand. Those foreign people, those English money-lenders, gave us gold and silver, and we propose to pay them back in the same money they gave us.

Let me say to you that the statement that silver has fallen is not sustained by the facts. A pound of silver to-day buys as much wheat, buys as much cotton, buys as much property and buys as much labor as it ever did, and buys as much as it did when we got that money. It is gold, the gold dollar, that has gone up to where it buys twice as much as it formerly did.

These debts my fellow citizens, cannot be paid for centuries, and shall we now declare that our people must go on paying interest, paying principal, with 200-cent dollars, or shall we go back and say we will pay in 100-cent dollars? Shall we pay in the same kind of money they gave us? But these English money-lenders and their American agents and representatives do not intend to give up the advantage they have gained. The bond holders are now making fortunes and won't let go. They are making a determined fight to perpetuate low prices. Two weeks ago they went to St. Louis and took charge of the Republican convention, an assembly that will go into history as "Mark Hanna's Trust." At that convention Mr. Hanna nominated a candidate for President; a candidate with one idea, and that idea wrong. That convention declared in favor of the present English single gold standard. The London newspapers have complimented that convention and that platform. They are delighted with it. An Englishman always feels good when he sees a prospect of getting more sweat and more blood out of the American people. To be sure, they said nothing about a tariff in that platform, but the moneyed people cared nothing about that; they knew that was simply a little dough intended to hide the hook.

Now, after they have harnessed the Republican party to the English cart, the other members of the firm are here trying to put the same English halter upon this convention. Are you going to allow them to do it? What are the arguments that you hear around the hotels and at your headquarters? You noticed some weeks ago these Eastern people declared that they would have nothing but a single gold standard, but when they found that the people were against them—when they found that the Democracy of the country would not tolerate it, then they were willing to modify their demands. They have come on here and are talking compromise. "Get together and agree upon something that we can all accede to and endorse," is what they now say.

We are asked to do as we have done in the past. We are asked to adopt a declaration of principle which will mean one thing to one man and another to another man; which will mean one thing in one section of the country and another thing in another section, and which will enable these people to maintain a single gold standard in the end.

These forces are powerful. They represent the bankers of London and control nearly all of the banks throughout the country. A few banks in London and New York to-day control the whole banking system of this country. They control all of the newspapers, all of the agents that formulate thought; they control the corporations—the manufacturer and the merchant, and we have recently had something like a monetary terrorism. Anyone who did not subscribe to their wishes was threatened with social, financial and political death. Catch phrases are invented. There was a time in the history of the world when men and women were slaughtered in the name of liberty. We have seen a time when a great nation can be robbed in the name of an honest dollar. There are men who otherwise are intelligent and seem patriotic, who claim that they love their country, who yet are doing all they can to fasten this English yoke upon our people.

The question now is shall the Democratic party stand squarely for liberty, or shall we straddle, shall we dodge? Shall we put ourselves in the position of the steer which jumped part way over the fence and could neither hook before nor kick behind?

Gentlemen, there is a principle involved here which rises above vote getting, which rises above office getting—a principle which affects the welfare of a great nation. In 1776 the question was, Shall republican institutions be established in America? In 1896 the question is, Shall republican institutions be perpetuated in America? Or shall we make the mass of the toilers and producers of this country mere vassals, mere tribute-paying serfs to English capitalists? Shall we install the typical Johnny Bull, with whip in hand, as a task-master over all the generations of Americans yet to come? That is the question. England devours the substance of Ireland; she gathers the harvest in the valley of the Nile; she has carried away the riches of India; she has ravished the islands of the sea; she has drawn the life blood out of every people that has ever come under her domination. Shall this mighty nation, after we have triumphed over English armies upon land, after we have destroyed English fleets upon the waters, after we have triumphed upon every field of honor and field of glory—shall we now supinely surrender to English greed, English cunning, and English corruption?

We must make no mistakes. Our people are in earnest. They will have neither straddling on platform or straddling on candidate, and those prudent, cautious, wise gentlemen, who have to consult the tin roosters every morning to see what their convictions should be during the day can have no show in this convention.

We must have a declaration of principles that will admit of no quibble. We must have a declaration of principles that will mean the same thing on the mountain, in the valley, and at the seashore. We must have a declaration of principles that we can hold up before all Israel and the sun.

It is not the time for compromise. It is a time to be serious, because the question is serious. It involves the future of our country. If the present standard of value, the present standard of prices, is to be maintained, then the great producing classes of this country will be devoured by the fixed charges. They will have no money to buy the comforts of life. They will have no money to educate their families. It is not a question that can be compromised. Compromise is proper when it involves only personal interest, but not when the interests of a great nation are at stake.

Just see how history repeats itself. In 1776 the money classes in our country were opposed to the Declaration of Independence. They represented foreign interest, and they talked compromise. In 1861 the money classes of the East were opposed to making great sacrifices to maintain the Union. They talked compromise.

In 1896 the same interests are again represented, and they talk compromise.

My fellow-citizens, the hand of compromise never yet ran up the flag of freedom. The spirit of compromise never yet laid the foundations of republican institutions. No compromise army ever fought the battles of liberty. Go search the hundred thousand graves found on hilltop, found in forests and in fields, where sleep the men who died to uphold this flag, and you will not find the bones of a single man that talked compromise. They stood erect and said to the Almighty, "Here are our lives."

Gentlemen, the time has come when the Democratic party must announce to the world that we stand for great principles, that we stand for those principles that offer hope to humanity, and that we offer our lives to defend them. To simply say that we are Democrats may sound laconic, but unless we stand for something definite that earnest men and earnest women can lay hold on in life, unless we stand for something that will lift up humanity, we will be despised by mankind. And if this convention will rise to the occasion, as I believe it will, if this convention will rise to meet the needs of a great people, then our morning will be wrapped in splendor. If we do that, then the ides of November will usher in a new century of prosperity, of industry, of enterprise, and of happiness. It will usher in a century which in grandeur and in glory will surpass all that have gone before.

ADDRESS ON LABOR UNREST AND
THE PULLMAN STRIKE

Delivered at New York, October 17, 1896

To answer his critics and take his case to the nation, Altgeld journeyed
eastward to deliver a national address at Cooper Union in New York
City. An address of great length, it presented a fully documented
defense of Altgeld's policies concerning the Pullman strike and his
struggle with the Federal administration of President Grover A.
Cleveland. The address also ranged over other significant issues of
the day.

I have come to bring to the patriotic people of New York
and of the East the greeting of the great Mississippi Valley; of
that hardy yeomanry of the Central and Western States that
has always rallied to the support of the American flag in times of
danger, and that supports and maintains our institutions in times
of peace. Those great toiling and producing masses who make
our civilization possible feel that their destiny is linked with that
of the sons of liberty who inhabit the East. We are unwilling to
believe out in the West that patriotism has died east of the
Alleghenies and that Mammon is the only·god at whose shrine
Eastern people bow. We are unwilling to believe that the few
men in your large cities who use government as a convenience to
make fortunes; who use our republic as a mere foraging ground
to amass wealth; who cringe to European aristocracy and who

wave the American flag with one hand while robbing the public with the other, represent the sentiment of that section of the country that was the cradle of American liberty. We do not believe that because you have in your midst men who value the privilege of taking breakfast with the Prince of Wales more than they do the blessings of free government; that because you have in your midst men who are ready to undermine and to overthrow republican institutions in our land in order to gain a temporary personal advantage for themselves, that therefore the fires of liberty which for more than a century burned upon your hilltops and illumined the world are extinct. We believe that the hearts of a majority of your people are loyal to the institutions of the fathers, and that they beat in unison with the hearts of the great people of the South and West who believe that the time has not come for converting this republic into an oligarchy.

THE MODERN EUMENIDES

At present there is in addition to the gold standard a quartette of blighting sisters in our land, respectively called:
"Federal interference in local affairs."
"Government by injunction."
"Usurpation by the United States Supreme Court," and fourth, "Corruption."
All four are clothed in phariseeism and pretense, and all recognize the gold standard as their natural or foster mother. We believe that these blighting sisters whose smile means paralysis and whose embrace means death have no more admirers among your people than they have among ours.

This campaign is to decide, not only whether we shall perpetuate the experiments of this English financial system, which is prostrating our nation, but also whether we shall permanently adopt these four sisters into our household and make them the ruling members of the family.

THE GOLD STANDARD DISASTROUS

The mask has been torn from the gold standard. Our people are beginning to understand the attempt to introduce it throughout the commercial world is a disastrous experiment; that down to 1873 the world used not only all the gold and all the silver as money, but so great was the world's business that every dollar was loaded with twenty times as much credit; that all the great achievements of mankind were accomplished under the bi-metallic system; that under this system everything that makes the civilization of this century was done, and that since the introduction of the universal gold standard the wheels of progress have stood still. Our people are beginning to understand that formerly there was added every year to the world's stock of money, nearly all of the gold and silver that was mined, which in a measure kept pace with the increase of population, but that since 1873 only the gold has been added, that is, only one-half as much has been added each year as there formerly was, while the population has increased more rapidly than ever, and that this fact alone must produce a continuous fall in prices. Our people are beginning to understand that making money scarce makes money dear, that dear money means low prices for prop-erty, for the products of the earth and for the products of labor. They further understand that as taxes and debts were not re-duced low prices have destroyed the purchasing power of the farming and producing classes, so that they can no longer buy the products of the factory and the mill as they formerly did, in consequence of which the factory and the mill had to partially or wholly shut down, thus in turn destroying the purchasing power of the laborer, and that in this manner the gold standard has spread paralysis not only over America but over Europe and the civilized world. Our people understand that when the govern-ments of the earth forced the world off of the bimetallic standard of prices down onto the low gold standard prices, they practic-ally doubled the burden of all debtors, and that strange as it may seem none of the pharisees who now cry aloud against making money cheap and injuring the creditor ever uttered a word of sympathy for the poor debtor. They understand that the bullion in one of the so-called "fifty-cent dollars"—treated as bullion with the stamp of the government erased—has substanti-ally the same purchasing power and will buy as much property, as much of the products of the earth and of labor, as had or did any of the dollars which the Englishmen gave us for our bonds. They understand that the gold dollar has been forced up to where it will buy twice as much property and products as it formerly did; that the governments by destroying silver reduced the world's supply of money and by making gold alone do the world's work they increased the demand for it, thus interfering with the law of supply and demand, and that as soon as this legislation is wiped out gold will of necessity come down to its former position. Our people understand that it will be impossible to open the mills and restore prosperity to the world until the purchasing power of the farming and the great producing classes of the earth is restored and that this can only be done by putting an end to this gold standard experiment and restoring bimetallism.

REPUBLICAN ABUSE AND VILIFICATION

Finding that the facts and the arguments were against them the gold standard people are resorting to vilification and abuse, a specimen of which has lately been furnished the people of the West by a triplet of retired generals drawing high salaries, who have been giving exhibitions under the management, and, as I am informed, under the care of Mr. Hanna, and who showed in their first efforts that they did not know the one-hundredth part as much about the money question as did the poor privates whom they were seeking to convert. But what they lacked in knowledge on the money question they made up in abuse. They carried with them a flat car built by Mr. Pullman for this purpose, having on it a cannon and other military equipments, to show the laboring men of this country what policy they may reasonably expect to be carried out in case Mr. Hanna succeeds in carrying this election.

Now, my fellow-citizens, let me direct your attention to that part of the Chicago platform which denounces what I have called "The Blighting Sisters." Calamities rarely come singly. Whenever the foundation is undermined a horde of evils follow and there has come upon us a group of evils, each one of which is destructive of republican institutions. If they were not born of, they at least came hand in hand with this English system of low prices and great debts. Poverty and loss of liberty go together. The forces which produce the one generally build the machinery that destroys the other.

FEDERAL INTERFERENCE

Let us look at "Federal Interference and Government by Injunction," and to illustrate how the Constitution and the laws can be trampled upon and every principle of free government brushed away with a mere wave of the hand, I will cite the action of the federal government and the federal courts during the railroad strike in 1894. I am aware that by persistent vilification and deliberate misrepresentation the partisan press has made the impression upon the minds of many good citizens that I, as Governor of Illinois, during the railroad disturbances of two years ago, did not do my duty and did not make the proper effort to protect life and property in Chicago, but sympathized with lawlessness and disorder; that federal interference was necessary to save the city. If there were even a semblance of truth in this, then no condemnation could be too severe, for a government that will not promptly and thoroughly protect life and property and preserve law and order is an abomination and should be wiped off of the earth. But, let us see what the indisputable facts are as shown by the records, and then you can judge for yourselves.

A narration of the incidents in that strike at Chicago may be a little tedious, but as it bears on one of the great issues of this campaign and shows what the laboring classes of this country may expect for themselves and their children if the present tendency is not arrested, it is important.

THE COAL STRIIKE

In order to give you a more comprehensive view of the situation, I remind you that during the several months immediately prior to the beginning of the railroad strike there prevailed in all of the coal mining States a great coal miners' strike, which was so serious that it stopped production and in some localities caused a coal famine. The policy of the miners was to abstain from work until a standard of wages could be fixed. Their families were in great distress and never did men behave better or show themselves to be better law-abiding citizens than did nearly all of the miners during that time. Illinois has one of the largest coal fields in the world—a coal field 250 miles long and over 100 miles wide, and there are coal mines all over it. The suspension of mining extended nearly all over the State. As a rule the miners themselves were well behaved, but disorderly elements in some cases taking advantage of the situation attempted to interfere with the moving of trains, and in several instances by stealthy acts, and without the knowledge or even the suspicion of the local civil officers, succeeded in committing depredations. During this strike there was a demand for troops from various sections of the State, and they were not only furnished promptly, but they were moved with a celerity never exceeded by the regular army. The Illinois National Guard consists of about 6,000 men, and in point of training, readiness for duty, soldierly bearing and general intelligence, they are not surpassed by any body of soldiers on this continent. During this coal strike troops were sent to six or eight different points in the State. Frequently the request for them did not come in until 11 o'clock at night and the order for troops to report at a particular point was issued at that late hour, and in such perfect control was the guard, and so perfect were the arrangements for collecting men that in instances of this character, where they did not receive the order until midnight, they got together and were moved 100 miles and reported for duty by sunrise in the morning at the place of trouble. In several instances an entire regiment reported for duty at a point 240 miles from its headquarters within 14 hours after it was ordered out. During that long strike order was maintained everywhere, railroad trains were moved, and in those instances where depredations had been committed stealthily the offenders were all arrested and immediately lodged in jail and were punished.

An examination of the records will show that while during the coal strikes some of the railroads in Ohio, were Major McKinley was Governor, were almost paralyzed and were at the mercy of the mobs in some cases for nearly a week at a time, in Illinois they got instant relief.

THE RAILROAD STRIKE

No sooner was this coal strike over than the great railroad strike began, and the operatives or trainmen of nearly all the great railroads of the country stopped work. This left the railroads helpless. Illinois is the greatest railroad State in the

Union and Chicago the greatest railroad center in the world. The operating and switching yards of that city were mostly out on the prairie adjoining the city and were so extensive as to almost surround it. In addition to Chicago there are more than a dozen railroad centers scattered over the State. The railroad operatives, partly out of respect for the law and partly because they felt that violence would injure their cause, were orderly, but in centers of population, where there were great numbers of idle men drawn together by the excitement, a vicious element sometimes became demonstrative, and after the roads succeeded in getting new men to man some of their trains there were efforts made by the mob to prevent the moving of Pullman cars, and this in some cases precipitated trouble. Under the laws of Illinois, whenever the civil authorities are not able to maintain order or enforce the law, the Governor can order out troops for their assistance on the application of either the sheriff of the county, the mayor of a city or village, the county judge or the coroner. The constitution and laws of that State, in harmony with the Constitution and laws of the federal government, are based upon the principle that in a republic in time of peace the military should be subject to the civil officers and that the maintenance of law and order should in the first instance devolve upon the local officers in each community.

Early in this railroad strike and before there had been any serious disturbances in Chicago, applications for assistance were made by the local civil officers of five or six different railroad centers throughout the State and troops were promptly sent to their assistance, always arriving on the ground within a few hours after they had been applied for.

STATE TROOPS PROMPTLY FURNISHED

To show the attitude of the State administration during this time, I quote a few dispatches received and sent, which are fair specimens of all. On July 1, I received a dispatch from Decatur, Ill., signed by a number of passengers on a railroad train stating that no effort was being made by the railroad company to move their train and they demanded assistance. This was the first intimation that I had that there was any trouble in that locality, and I immediately sent this telegram to the sheriff of that county:

Springfield, July 1, 1894.

To the Sheriff of Macon County, Decatur, Ill.:

I have a dispatch purporting to come from passengers now detained at Decatur because trains are obstructed and they ask for assistance. Wire me the situation fully. Are railroad officials making proper efforts to move trains and are you able to furnish the traveling public the necessary protection and to enforce the law?

J. P. ALTGELD, Governor.

To this the sheriff replied that he had been able to preserve order so far, but could do so no longer, and asked for troops, and the following reply was sent:

Springfield, July 1, 1894.

To the Sheriff of Macon County, Decatur, Ill.:

Have ordered troops to your assistance. They should reach you before sunrise. See that all trains unlawfully held are released at once.

J. P. ALTGELD, Governor.

On the same day the Chicago & Eastern Illinois Railroad Company telegraphed from Danville that their trains were tied up at that point and that the sheriff would do nothing, although he had had been repeatedly called on, and they asked for assistance. To this the following reply was sent:

Springfield, July 1, 1894.

W. H. Lyford, General Counsel, C. & E. I. R. R. Co.:

We can furnish assistance promptly if the civil authorities show that they need it. Thus far there has been no application for assistance from any of the officials of Vermilion county, either sheriff, coroner, mayor of town or the county judge.

J. P. ALTGELD, Governor.

At the same time the following dispatch was sent to the sheriff of Vermilion county:

Springfield, July 1, 1894.

To the Sheriff of Vermilion County, Danville, Ill.:

Officials of the Eastern Illinois Railroad complain that their trains have been tied up and that they cannot get sufficient protection to move them. Please wire me the situation fully. Can you enforce the law and protect the traveling public with such force as you can command?

J. P. ALTGELD, Governor.

A similar telegram was at the same time sent to the county

judge and other local officers. The following reply was received from the sheriff:

Danville, Ill., July 1, 1894.

Governor J. P. Altgeld:

Your message received. Send me one hundred rifles and ammunition and I will try to protect the railroad's men and property. As to the situation, there are from 300 to 700 men on the ground and oppose the movement of any and all trains or cars except mail cars. They are usually quiet and duly sober, but are very determined. I will advise if I am not able to afford protection.

J. W. NEWTON, Sheriff.

To this the following telegram was sent:

Springfield, July 1, 1894.

To J. A. Newton, Sheriff, Danville, Ill.:

We have not got 100 stand of arms left here, but from information we get we consider situation serious at Danville, and therefore have sent you troops. They will be there early in the morning. All those trains unlawfully held should be moved before noon.

J. P. ALTGELD, Governor.

OLNEY STATES THE CORRECT DOCTRINE

In several instances troops had been asked for to protect railroad property and were promptly furnished, and it was then found that the railroad companies had no men who were willing to work, and we had to find soldiers who had to act as brakemen and engineers in order to transport the troops. Several weeks prior to these dates, while the coal strike was pending, the Hon. William J. Allen, United States District Judge at Springfield, Ill., finding that the marshal was having trouble to carry out some of the orders of his court, wrote to the Attorney General at Washington upon the subject of receiving assistance from federal troops to enforce the orders of the United States court, and the Attorney General sent the following dispatch:

Washington, D.C., June 16, 1894.

Allen, United States Judge, Springfield, Illinois:

I understand the State of Illinois is willing to protect property against lawless violence with military force if necessary. Please advise receivers to take proper steps to procure protection by civil authorities of the State. If such protection proved inadequate, the government should be applied to for military assistance.

OLNEY, Attorney General.

This laid down the correct doctrine, that is, that the local authorities should be applied to first, and in case of their failure, then the Governor of the State should be applied to for assistance. Immediately after the date of this telegram, and on several occasions thereafter during the coal strike, as well as on several occasions during the subsequent railroad strike, prior to the serious disturbances in Chicago, the United States Marshal for the Southern District of Illinois applied to the Governor for military aid to enable him and his deputies to execute the processes of the United States court, and in each instance troops were promptly sent to his assistance. This, in brief, shows the attitude of the State administration toward that part of the State lying outside of Chicago, and as troops were always promptly furnished where needed, and in every instance were promptly furnished to the United States Marshal when asked for to assist him in enforcing the orders of the United States court for Southern Illinois, and as the State administration stood equally ready to furnish any assistance which the United States Marshal at Chicago might require to carry out the orders of the United States court there, and inasmuch as Attorney General Olney had only a few weeks before telegraphed that the Governor should be applied to for troops to assist in carrying out the orders of the United States court, it would naturally be expected that if the United States Marshal at Chicago should need assistance that he would apply for such assistance to the Governor of the State. But instead of pursuing this course, just the opposite course was pursued. No application of any sort for troops was made to the Governor by the United States Marshal or any of the United States authorities at Chicago, nor was any such application made by any of the local city or county officers of Chicago until the 6th of July, and then such application was made on my suggestion.

You may ask why the federal administration at Washington did not direct the United States Marshal at Chicago to apply to the State for troops in order to enforce the orders of the United States courts there just as the United States Marshal for Southern Illinois had applied to the State for troops to enforce the orders of the United States courts at that place? I will tell you. It subsequently developed that more than ten days before there was any trouble the corporations of Chicago applied to the federal government for troops so that a precedent might be set under which they could in the future appeal directly in all cases to the federal government and become independent of local governments.

OLNEY REVERSES HIMSELF

Thereupon, more than five days in advance of any trouble in Chicago, Mr. Olney and Mr. Cleveland decided to reverse the policy and practice of the government and take an entire new departure by setting a precedent of having the President to interfere at pleasure and having the United States courts and the United States government take the corporations directly under their wings in the first instance in all cases, and in order to have the American people submit to the violation of the Constitution and laws of the land as well as of every principle of self-government, the trouble at Chicago was, by systematic effort and deliberate misrepresentation, so magnified as to make it seem that we were bordering on anarchy, and that consequently federal interference was necessary. The impression was sought to be made upon the country that we were bordering on civil war and the destruction of society and that neither the local authorities nor the State authorities were willing to maintain law and order, while the real fact was that the federal government took steps to interfere in Chicago before there was any rioting or any serious trouble of any kind, and that the State authorities, who stood ready to act promptly, were intentionally ignored.

THE DESTRUCTION NOT GREAT

The disturbance at its worst did not equal in point of destructiveness the disturbances that occurred at Buffalo, N.Y., the year previous; was not near so bloody or destructive as a number of disturbances that have occurred in Pennsylvania, and was not as bloody or destructive as had occurred in Ohio while Mr. McKinley was Governor.

The federal commission appointed by President Cleveland afterwards to investigate this strike made a thorough examination of the subject and in its report used this language:

"According to the testimony the railroads lost in property destroyed and in the hire of United States deputy marshals and other incidental expenses at least $685,783.00."

Bear in mind that this includes the expense of a large number of deputy marshals and of loss sustained, as the commission says, in other incidental expenses. Deducting this incidental expense and the part that was paid deputy marshals and it reduces the amount of property actually destroyed to a sum which is lower thar the amount that was destroyed in the disturbances in the other States that I have mentioned, and when it is remembered that property destroyed consisted chiefly of freight cars found in railroad yards that extended over miles of territory and that it was easy for lawless men to stealthily set cars on fire under this situation, it will be seen that the property destroyed by actual rioting or by a large mob was very small. The Chicago Fire Deparment, which officially investigated every case where there was a car or any other property destroyed, reports as follows: "During the first three days of the month of July no efforts were made to damage the property of corporations. After that the destruction of property was as follows:

July 4th	$ 2,150
July 5th	3,435
July 6th	338,972
July 7th	3,700
July 8th	575
July 9th	1,150
July 10th	850
July 11th	2,100
July 12th	565
July 13th	115
July 14th	2,300
Total	$355,612

Subsequent examinations have shown that even this sum was exaggerated. It will be seen by the table that nearly all of this occurred on the 6th of July and was due to the fact that a fire had broken out in a very large railroad yard south of the city, where there was no water and where the fire department was consequently powerless. It seems that most of the burning occurred in the evening after the rioting of that day in that locality had been suppressed, and after both the police and the State troops had arrived on the ground, but owing to the absence of water but little could be done to arrest the flames. One fire engine put out over a half a mile of hose, but was unable then to reach the cars. A mere glance at the facts shows that the reports that were sent out as to the actual conditions in Chicago during the strike were malicious libels upon the city.

It will be noticed, according to the reports of the fire department, that it was not until the 4th of July that the rioting began, and it was very light during the 4th and 5th of July and did not become serious until the 6th.

So much for the extent of the riot.

EFFECT OF STRIKE ON MAIL SERVICE

Now let us see how it affected the mail service. Several months after the riot the superintendent of the railway mail service at Chicago, upon whom the duty of getting the mails in and out of Chicago during the strike devolved, wrote as follows in regard to the extent of the delays:

With the exception of some trains that were held at Hammond, Ind., Washington Heights, Danville and Cairo, Ill., the greatest delay to any of the outgoing and incoming mails probably did not exceed from eight to nine hours at any time.

Louis L. Troy, Superintendent.

This shows that whatever the difficulties may have been at other points there were no great delays at Chicago, and when it is remembered that the railroads for a time were helpless because they could not get men to man their trains, it is apparent that the delays there were very insignificant, and that in so far as the mails are concerned nothing had happened to call for federal interference. The truth is that there had been strikes in Chicago that looked more formidable than this one and yet the mayor and local authorities had found themselves amply able to preserve order and enforce the law. In the present case the mayor had sworn in a large number of extra policemen, and the sheriff of the county had sworn in a large number of deputy sheriffs, and they believed themselves to be able to easily control the situation. Early in the trouble, Sheriff Gilbert, who was a Republican, telegraphed for arms with which to equip his deputies, and these arms were at once sent him. This was the last request he ever made for assistance.

Remember, now, that the report of the fire department shows that on the 1st, 2d and 3d of July there was no property destroyed; that on the 4th and on the 5th of July there was a little destruction of property, and it was not until the 6th of July that the rioting became serious. I call your attention to the following:

"On the afternoon of June 30 the superintendent of the railway mail service at Chicago sent the following dispatch to the authorities at Washington: 'No mails have accumulated at Chicago so far. All regular trains are moving nearly on time with a few slight exceptions.

LEWIS L. TROY, Superintendent.' "

Yet notwithstanding this dispatch, on the next morning, before anything more had happened, the authorities at Washington decided to appoint a special attorney at Chicago to represent the United States in the strike. Thus far it will be noticed that the government was in no way involved. It had just been advised there was no serious delay in the mails and there was nothing in the situation that in any way affected the federal government.

INTERESTED ATTORNEY APPOINTED SPECIAL COUNSEL

The government already had a United States District Attorney with a large number of assistants in that city who were amply able to attend to all of the government business there, but instead of simply increasing their number, Attorney General Olney and President Cleveland decided to appoint a special counsel who should still more directly represent the government during this strike. The administration claimed to be Democratic. There were hundreds of able and distinguished Democratic lawyers in Chicago whose appointment would have carried confidence, but the administration would not have any of these. The Attorney General and the President evidently felt that when the Constitution and the laws were to be trampled on, when the precedents and traditions of the government were to be disregarded and a new and a revolutionary policy was to be inaugurated, that they needed a Republican for that purpose. Here again there were hundreds of able and distinguished Republican lawyers in Chicago who were not connected with corporations, who were in no way involved in the strike on either side and whose appointment would at least have aroused no suspicion; but the Attorney General and the President evidently felt that they would not do; that for the particular work which they wanted done they needed a corporation lawyer, and here again there were a large number of able and distinguished corporation lawyers in Chicago who were Republicans and who were in no way involved in the strike on either side; but the Attorney General and the President evidently felt that for the peculiar and revolutionary work they wanted done these men might not be reliable. So they rejected these and appointed Mr. Walker, who was not only a Republican and a corporation lawyer, but who was at that time the attorney for a great railroad that was directly involved in the strike, so that he himself was already involved in the controversy, he on one side and the railroad employes on the other. In other words the Attorney General and the President took one of the parties to the controversy and placed at his disposal United States Marshals, United States courts and the United States army. Never before in the history of our country were the courts, the grand juries, the United States Marshals and the United States army stripped of all semblance of impartiality and given as a convenience to one of the parties.

This, bear in mind, was on the first day of July, three days ahead of any rioting and five days in advance of any serious rioting, and on the same day the United States troops at Fort Sheridan, within an hour's run of Chicago, were ordered to be in readiness to go to that city on a moment's notice. The plan determined upon was to have the United States courts issue blanket injunctions, hereafter explained, against the strikers and all other people, forbidding everything imaginable, and then use the marshals for the purpose of carrying out these injunctions and use the federal troops for this and other purposes. Up to this time neither the Republican sheriff of the county nor Mr. Hopkins, the Democratic mayor of the city, nor any other local State official, nor any federal official at Chicago or elsewhere had applied to the Governor for troops.

PERVERSION OF INTERSTATE COMMERCE LAW

Some of the judges who issued these injunctions claimed to base them upon what was called the Interstate Commerce Law, an act of Congress passed some years ago for the purpose of protecting the shippers of this country, and especially for the purpose of preventing unjust discrimination by the railroads between shippers. This act had become almost inoperative so far as the purpose of its enactment was concerned, because some of these same judges had first held one clause and then another clause to be unconstitutional, so that it was practically destroyed as a measure that should prevent discrimination by the railroads. But after having rendered it harmless so far as the railroads were concerned at that time (the Supreme Court has since reversed some of their decisions) they, to the amazement of the American people, made of this law a club with which to pound the backs of the laboring men. I repeat that some of the judges based their injunctions on the ground of protecting interstate commerce, and they held that if a car was loaded with goods at any point and was intended to be shipped to some point out of the State, that then it was interstate commerce and the President and the federal authorities could take complete control of the situation and could ignore State and local authorities entirely. Some of these injunctions were sued out by the Attorney General in the name of the United States, and were claimed to be partly based on the anti-trust law, an act of Congress intended to prevent the formation of trusts by large corporations in restraint of trade. The Attorney General had refused to enforce this law. He did not try to break up a single trust under it, but after having refused to enforce it against the corporations and for the purpose for which it was passed, he made it a whip with which to scourge labor.

CALL FOR FEDERAL TROOPS UNWARRANTED

Immediately after the beginning of the strike in which the railway operatives refused to work, the managers of the railway lines entering Chicago formed an organization to fight the strike, and they met towards the close of each day to report upon the situation, and at 6 o'clock p.m. of July 2, the day after the special counsel had been appointed by the government, and the day after the troops at Fort Sheridan had been ordered to be in readiness at Chicago, they met and reported as to the condition of their roads and the following copies of reports made by themselves, which are samples of all the reports, show the situation at that time:

Wisconsin Central: "All passenger and freight trains moving and business resumed its normal condition."

Chicago & Northern Pacific: "Suburban trains all running about on time. Freight moving without interruption. Night suburban trains discontinued for fear of being stoned by loafers."

Chicago, Burlington & Quincy: "Thirty-seven car loads of dressed beef loaded in Kansas City yesterday morning have passed over this road safely and delivered to Eastern lines this afternoon and are now moving all right."

Chicago, Milwaukee & St. Paul: "All passenger trains have arrived and departed on time. No freight moving here, but is moving on other parts of the line."

Chicago & Northwestern: "All through passenger traffic has been continued without interruption. Not trying to handle freight."

Lake Shore & Michigan Southern: "No interruption to business. Both passenger and freight trains have come and departed as usual."

Baltimore & Ohio: "All passenger trains with full equipment met with no delay and all very nearly on time."

Chicago and Great Western: "Passenger trains moving as usual with regular Pullman equipment. Freight service partially resumed on the Chicago Division."

Chicago & Erie: "All passenger trains are running out on time. Not attempting to do freight business. Have trouble at Marion, O."

This was on the evening of July 2d, and corroborates the statement made by the fire department that for the first three days in July no attempt was made to destroy railroad property. In those cases where a road was not attempting to move freight it was due to the fact that their old hands had quit work and they had not yet been able to get new ones.

On the morning of July 3d, being the morning after the railroad managers had reported the conditions of their roads, as already shown, and before anything further had developed, Mr. Walker, the special counsel, dictated a dispatch which was sent to Washington, asking that federal troops be sent into the city, and on the afternoon of the 3d, the federal troops appeared in Chicago and camped on the Lake Front and ostensibly went on duty. Let me repeat here that up to this time there had been no serious disturbance of mails, no destruction of property and according to the reports of the railroad managers themselves no serious interference with the operation of the railroads or with interstate commerce.

STATE AUTHORITIES IGNORED

And let me also repeat that up to this time the State and local authorities had been completely ignored, the State was not asked to do anything or to assist in any manner, although it was not only able to entirely control the situation, but stood ready to do it. The special counsel for the government was also the representative of the railroads, and assistance from the State was not wanted, but every step was taken to establish a new precedent that might be used in the future; that is, to apply only to the federal government so that the corporations might at any time in the future be able to get federal troops at pleasure and also that the precedent might be established of authorizing the President to interfere at pleasure in any community, because if interstate commerce is to embrace any car or any article of merchandise intended to be shipped out of the State, then there is scarcely a neighborhood in America but what some pretext could be found for sending federal troops into it.

At about 6 o'clock on the evening of July 3d, about the time the United States troops were entering Chicago, the managers of the different railroads again met and reported in substance as follows:

Santa Fe: "Six regular passenger trains on time; moving freight."

Chicago, Milwaukee & St. Paul: "All passengers on time and without interference; moving freight."

Chicago & Alton: "Trains stop for want of firemen."

Baltimore & Ohio: "Trains moving; one engine detached by

withdrawal of coupling pin; police detailed and protected train at once."

Chicago, Burlington & Quincy: "Passenger trains running as usual; no freight handled because firemen and engineers refused to work with new men."

Lake Shore & Michigan Southern: "Trains moving as usual; freight trains delayed at Englewood, but prompt action by the police department raised the blockade."

Chicago & Eastern Illinois: "Situation better than yesterday."

Illinois Central: "Ties found on track nearing crossing, but did not delay trains; matters getting along as nicely as could be expected under the circumstances."

Chicago & Great Western: "Passenger trains all moving; freight trains started; went through without trouble."

Chicago & Grand Trunk: "Completely blockaded at Battle Creek, Michigan; will send out no trains from Chicago until that is raised."

Monon Route: "Men cannot be had to take strikers' places."

Chicago & Erie: "Passenger trains moving all right on time."

Wabash: "Account of trouble at other places, but none at Chicago."

Panhandle: "Trains moving all right, none more than twenty minutes late."

Chicago & Northern Pacific: "All day suburban trains on time; business being handled without interruption."

Rock Island: "Trouble at Des Moines, Iowa, at Blue Island and at other places, but none at Chicago."

On the 4th day of July there was some disturbance, although the federal troops were on the ground, but instead of overawing the mob they seemed to act only as an irritant to intensify the situation, and on the evening of the 4th of July the managers again met and reported in substance as follows:

Chicago & Alton: "Local trains between Chicago, Joliet and Dwight are running; through trains are held at Bloomington by strikers."

Santa Fe: "Everything in pretty good shape; passenger trains on time; ran five freight trains in Missouri and eleven in Illinois in past twenty-four hours and have resumed local freight service between Chicago and Streator."

Chicago, Milwaukee & St. Paul: "Trouble with firemen running on Council Bluffs line; with the exception of a local train all passenger trains departed and arrived on time; no trouble on the line between Chicago and St. Paul."

Baltimore & Ohio: "Passenger trains on fairly good time; no delays due to strikers."

Nickel Plate: "Regular passenger trains left and arrived on time; freight switching business is at a standstill."

Chicago & Northwestern: "All through trains on Galena division gotten out last night, but suburban traffic on that division was hampered by inability to find engineers; are operating all passengers in and out of Chicago on Wisconsin division and are rapidly getting suburban traffic on Galena division running; handled no freight yesterday, but resumed to-day; brought in a train of fruit from the West and have several trains of beer coming in from Milwaukee; no acts of violence on our lines in city."

Wisconsin Central Lines: "Passenger and freight trains moving and about on time."

Chicago & Northern Pacific: "All suburban trains running regular except night trains; freight business is being handled promptly."

Michigan Central: "Handled all freight that is tendered; moving all trains and doing regular work; a train of beef consisting of forty cars which was held at Halsted street has been pulled through the jam and is moving eastward."

Illinois Central: "The conditions on this line are more favorable than since the beginning of the strike; there is no suburban service to-day, but this service will be resumed to-morrow morning; handled 109 cars of merchandise and coal yesterday placed on tracks for unloading."

Chicago & Eastern Illinois: "Moving some passenger trains and resuming business gradually."

Chicago & Grand Trunk: "Started out mail train for the East this morning; have no equipment at Chicago with which to make up through trains, as this is tied up by strikers at Battle Creek, Mich."

Chicago, Burlington & Quincy: "Had trouble in attempting to move a freight train; last night Pullman cars were cut from

passenger train, but with assistance of police were promptly re-
coupled and train moved forward; all other trains of last night
and to-day are running without interfetrence of any kind. The
entire force of switchmen in St. Louis left the service of the road
yesterday evening. We are not trying to handle freight to-day;
everything is quiet."

PROMPT RESPONSE TO CALL FOR STATE TROOPS

On the 5th of July the conditions were about the same as on
the 4th, but there were rumors of an extension of the strike,
and it is evident that the federal troops were doing no good
there. On the morning of the 6th of July the President of the
Illinois Central Railroad telegraphed me that the property of
his road was being destroyed by a mob and that he could not
get protection. I wired him at once to get some one of the local
authorities who are authorized to ask for troops to do so, and
that if all should refuse, to wire me that fact, and that we would
furnish protection promptly. I took the position as a matter of
law that if the local authorities failed to protect property and
enforce the law and refused to apply for State aid while property is actually being destroyed and the peace is being disturbed, that then the Governor of the State not only has the
right, but it is his duty to see that order is restored and the law
enforced, and therefore I sent that telegram. At the same time
I sent a telegram to a friend in Chicago requesting him to at
once see Mayor Hopkins and tell him that it seemed to me the
situation was serious and that he had better apply to the State
for aid. This message was at once communicated to Mayor Hopkins, and about noon on that day, being the 6th of July, the day
on which the property was destroyed, the mayor telegraphed
for troops and by sundown on that day we had put over 5,000
State troops on duty in Chicago, although some of them had to
be transported 150 miles to reach the city. Never were troops
moved with greater celerity. They at once got the situation under
control and stopped the rioting, but they found that one of the
railroad yards in which a fire had broken out was far out on
the prairie and had an insufficient supply of water; that the fire
department was unable to put out the fire and thus prevent the
destruction of some cars that took fire from others that were

burning. Within twenty-four hours after the State troops arrived on the ground the rioting was suppressed. There were still a few cases, during the following days, of stealthy incendiarism, but no more forcible resistance. On the morning of the 7th of July one of the companies of State troops was attacked by a large mob and opened fire on it and several men were killed.

Up to this time the United States Marshal at Chicago, instead of calling on the State for assistance, as the marshal for Southern Illinois had done, had sworn in an army of over 4,000 deputy marshals to assist him in carrying out the injunctions which had been issued by the courts. There was no trouble about enforcing the usual and regular processes of the United States court. The administration of justice was in no way interfered with, but this army of deputies was sworn in to carry out this new system of government known as government by injunction; but notwithstanding their number they did not seem able to accomplish anything. The disturbances kept growing and spreading. They were sent along lines of railroad which the federal courts had taken under their wing, but as already shown, it devolved in the end upon the police and State troops, the properly and regularly constituted authorities, to restore order.

FEDERAL TROOPS USELESS

Speaking of the work of the Federal troops in Chicago, it will be seen by the record that they did no good. They were ordered to be in readiness five days in advance of any trouble, and were actually on the ground on the 3d day of July, before there had been any serious disturbance of any kind, and they remained on the ground for weeks thereafter. Yet instead of overawing the mob or exerting an influence for good, their presence added to the excitement and served as an irritant, and instead of suppressing rioting it will be noticed that it did not begin until after their arrival and then grew steadily, and on the 6th, the worst day, instead of suppressing they accomplished nothing. The federal soldiers and their officers were no doubt brave men and good soldiers, but they, like the deputy marshals, were occupying an anomalous position, and were therefore under a disadvantage. I am informed that on one day they tried to move a freight train at the stock yards, but finally abandoned the attempt. So far as can be learned, their presence did not prevent the burning of a single freight car in Chicago, they accomplished nothing, yet during all this time the impression was made on the country that President Cleveland and the federal troops were saving Chicago, General Miles was in command, and his headquarters seemed to be, for a number of days, a regular newspaper bureau, and there was an apparent effort on the part of some people to make an impression throughout the East that civil war was raging in Chicago, and the General and President Cleveland vied with each other in claiming the credit of suppressing that war. Cleveland, whose star had been rapidly sinking, hoped to win glory enough to insure his reelection, and it is reported that a coldness has grown up between these gentlemen because they could not agree upon a division of the honors. The fact is that up to the time the State troops appeared upon the scene the police force of Chicago alone did all of any value that was done to maintain law and order.

The only officer who attempted to make any report of the things actually done by the federal troops in Chicago was Captain J. M. Lee, assistant to Inspector General (Exhibit C to report of Major General Nelson A. Miles to the Adjutant General United States Army, Sept. 4th, 1894). Captain Lee says that from July 4th to 20th he was constantly with the troops in Chicago. That duties consisted in communicating verbal orders and instructions of the commanding general to officers in command; also in accompanying troops to the riotous districts, selecting camps and stations and "in investigating and reporting upon the grave situations from day to day." It is clear that he would know of all that the troops did do. And as the whole report shows an effort to magnify every incident and make the most possible out of the occasion, we may feel certain that he told all he knew.

He tells of moving troops, etc., and that on the 5th of July at the stock yards "troops guarded a train, while loading with cattle, with loaded guns and fixed bayonets, one company on each side." That troops drove mob from in front of the engine and the train moved at noon. Track was obstructed by broken switch, which was repaired by railroad man, who was struck by a stone while doing this. That cars were overturned on track in advance of troops; that he accompanied railroad official to telegraph office to procure wrecking train, and then went east, where cars had been overturned on track, stopping trains; that by protection of two companies wreckage was removed and trains released. He does not say moved, simply released, and then he says: "Returned to where I had left cattle train, but obstructions had caused train to put back into the stock yards, and as a result of day's work here the strikers and mob were jubiliant over their success." Judging from his statement the entire job was abandoned and no further efforts were made. Certainly the federal troops did not put down the riot that day.

Then, in his record for July 6th, he says that he received report that passenger train was held on Grand Trunk Road at Forty-seventh street. Found trouble in getting any one to guide troops to the point, but finally got a guide and went ahead, and found that trouble had occurred at Fifty-first street; mob had been driven off and train released by Captain Conrad. Then he says: "At night observed fire of the burning of hundreds of freight cars about four miles southwest of stock yards." But he does not claim that the federal troops lifted a finger to prevent or to put out this fire. I have now given every specific thing named in his report that the federal troops actually did in Chicago. On the 5th their action, according to his report, encouraged the mob, and all that he claims for the 6th of July is that Captain Conrad had released a passenger train. This was the day on which so many freight cars burned. Yet, so far as appears from his report, the federal troops did not prevent the burning of one car or the ditching of a single engine. If they were there to protect property or commerce why did they not at least make an effort on that day?

Captain Lee next tells in his report of a trip to the town of Hammond, in the State of Indiana, where he says they arrived just in the nick of time to prevent rioting. How he knows this he does not say.

General Miles, in the report already referred to, does not mention anything in particular that the federal troops did. But after speaking of their discipline says: "And their actions have very greatly contributed to the maintenance of civil law and in my opinion saved this country from a serious rebellion when one had been publicly declared to exist by one most responsible for its existence." This is extraordinary language and in view of the fact that there was no disturbance whatever of any kind in the city proper, that the rioting was at the stock yards and in the railroad yards on the prairies on the outskirts of the city; in view of the comparatively small damage done as found by the federal commission appointed by President Cleveland to investigate the whole matter, and as also found by the Chicago fire department, and in view of the written statements of Louis L. Troy, the superintendent of mails, that there had at no time been any considerable delay in moving the mails; and in view of the written reports of the railroad managers themselves that there was comparatively little interruption of their business, and finally, in view of the report made by Captain Lee at the time this language of General Miles seems absurd and must tend to destroy confidence in his judgment or else create the conviction that he was trying to make a false impression for the sake of getting a little glory thereby.

It is a matter of gratification to every patriotic citizen of Illinois that it was the State troops and the local civil authorities that restored law and order in that city. While they were not petted by fashionable society and were given very stinted praise by the newspapers, they did deal directly with the mob and restored order. During the trouble thousands of men all over the State tendered their services to the Governor, and I am satisfied that an army of two hundred thousand men could have been mustered in a few days if they had been called for. This spirit of patriotism was especially manifested by the old soldiers of the State.

FORMAL PROTEST

On the 5th day of July, 1894, after the federal troops had gone on duty in Chicago, I sent the following protest to the President and asked him to remove the troops:

Executive Office, State of Illinois, July 5, 1894. Hon. Grover Cleveland, President of the United States, Washington, D.C.

Sir:—I am advised that you have ordered Federal troops to go into service in the State of Illinois. Surely the facts have not been correctly presented to you in this case, or you would not have taken this step, for it is entirely unnecessary, and, as it seems to me, unjustifiable. Waiving all questions of courtesy, I will say that the State of Illinois is not only able to take care of itself, but it stands ready to furnish the Federal government any assistance it may need elsewhere. Our military force is ample, and consists of as good soldiers as can be found in the country. They have been ordered promptly whenever and wherever they were needed. We have stationed in Chicago alone three Regiments of Infantry, one Battery and one troop of Cavalry, and no better soldiers can be found. They have been ready every moment to go on duty, and have been and are now eager to go into service, but they have not been ordered out because nobody in Cook county, whether official or private citizen, asked to have their assistance, or even intimated in any way that their assistance was desired or necessary.

So far as I have been advised, the local officials have been able to handle the situation. But if any assistance were needed, the State stood ready to furnish 100 men for every one man required, and stood ready to do so at a moment's notice. Notwithstanding these facts the Federal Government has been applied to by men who had political and selfish motives for wanting to ignore the State government. We have just gone through a long coal strike, more extensive here than in any other State, because our soft-coal field is larger than that of any other State. We have now had ten days of the railroad strike, and have promptly furnished military aid wherever the local officials needed it.

In two instances the United States marshal for the Southern District of Illinois applied for assistance to enable him to enforce the processes of the United Sttaes court, and troops were promptly furnished him, and he was assisted in every way he desired. The law has been thoroughly executed, and every man guilty of violating it during the strike has been brought to justice. If the marshal of the Northern District of Illinois or the authorities of Cook county needed military assistance they had but to ask for it in order to get it from the State.

At present some of our railroads are paralyzed, not by reason of obstruction, but because they cannot get men to operate their trains. For some reason they are anxious to keep this fact from the public, and for this purpose are making an outcry about obstructions in order to divert attention. Now, I will cite to you two examples which illustrate the situation:

Some days ago I was advised that the business of one of our railroads was obstructed at two railroad centers, and that there was a condition bordering on anarchy there, and I was asked to furnish protection so as to enable the employes of the road to operate the trains. Troops were promptly ordered to both points. Then it transpired that the company had not sufficient men on its line to operate one train. All the old hands were orderly, but refused to go to work. The company had large shops which worked a number of men who did not belong to the Railway Union and who could run an engine. They were appealed to to run the train but flatly refused. We were obliged to hunt up soldiers who could run an engine and operate a train. Again, two days ago, appeals which were almost frantic came from the officials of another road stating that at an important point on their line trains were forcibly obstructed, and that there was a reign of anarchy at that place, and they asked for protection so that they could move their trains. Troops were put on the ground in a few hours' time, when the officer in command telegraphed me that there was no trouble, and had been none at that point, but that the road seemed to have no men to run trains, and the sheriff telegraphed that he did not need troops, but would himself move every train if the company would only furnish an engineer. The result was that the troops were there twelve hours before a single train was moved, although there was no attempt at interference by anybody.

It is true that in several instances a road made efforts to work a few green men and a crowd standing around insulted them and tried to drive them away, and in a few other cases they cut off Pullman sleepers from trains. But all these troubles were local in character and could easily be handled by the State authorities. Illinois has more railroad men than any other State in the Union, but as a rule they are orderly and well-behaved. This is shown by the fact that so very little actual violence has been committed. Only a very small percentage of these men have been guilty of infractions of the law. The newspaper accounts have in many cases been pure fabrications and in others wild exaggerations.

I have gone thus into details to show that it is not soldiers that the railroads need so much as it men to operate trains, and that the conditions do not exist here which bring the cause within the Federal statutes, a statute that was passed in 1881 and was in reality a war measure. The statute authorized the use of Federal troops in a State whenever it shall be impracticable to enforce the laws of the United States within such States by the ordinary judicial proceedings. Such a condition does not exist in Illinois. There have been a few local disturbances, but nothing that seriously interfered with the administration of justice, or that could not be easily controlled by the local or State authorities, for the Federal troops can do nothing that the State troops cannot do.

I repeat that you have been imposed upon in this matter, but even if by a forced construction it were held that the conditions here came within the letter of the statute, then I submit that local self-government is a fundamental principle of our Constitution. Each community shall govern itself so long as it can and is ready and able to enforce the law, and it is in harmony with this fundamental principle that the statute authorizing the President to send troops into States must be construed; especially is this so in matter relating to the exercise. of the police power and the preservation of law and order.

To absolutely ignore a local government in matters of this kind, when the local government is ready to furnish assistance needed, and is amply able to enforce the law, not only insults the people of this State by imputing to them an inability to govern themselves, or an unwillingness to enforce the law, but is in violation of a basic principle of our institutions. The question of Federal supremacy is in no way involved. No one disputes it for a moment, but, under our Constitution, Federal supremacy and local self-government must go hand in hand, and to ignore the latter is to do violence to the Constitution.

As Governor of the State of Illinois, I protest against this, and ask the immediate withdrawal of the Federal troops from active duty in this State. Should the situation at any time get so serious that we cannot control it with the State forces, we will promptly ask for Federal assistance, but until such time, I protest, with all due deference, against this uncalled for reflection upon our people, and again ask the immediate withdrawal of these troops. I have the honor to be, yours respectfully,

JOHN P. ALTGELD, Governor of Illinois.

PRESIDENT'S REPLY

Executive Mansion, Washington, July 5, 1894.

Hon. John P. Altgeld, Governor of Illinois, Springfield, Ill.:

Sir:—Federal troops were sent to Chicago in strict accordance with the Constitution and laws of the United States, upon the demand of the postoffice department that obstruction of the mails should be removed, and upon the representations of the judicial officers of the United States that the process of the Federal courts could not be executed through the ordinary means, and upon competent proof that conspiracies existed against commerce between the States. To meet these conditions, which are clearly within the province of Federal authority, the presence of Federal troops in the city of Chicago was deemed not only proper, but necessary, and there has been no intention of thereby interfering with the plain duty of the local authorities to preserve the peace of the city.

GROVER CLEVELAND.

GOVERNOR ALTGELD'S SECOND TELEGRAM

To the Hon. Grover Cleveland, President of the United States, Washington, D.C.

Sir:—Your answer to my protest involves some startling conclusions and ignores and evades the question at issue—that is that the principle of local self-government is just as fundamental in our institutions as is that of Federal supremacy.

First—You calmly assume that the executive has the legal right to order Federal troops into any community of the United States, in the first instance, whenever there is the slightest disturbance, and that he can do this without any regard to the question as to whether that community is able to and ready to enforce the law itself, and, inasmuch as the executive is the sole judge of the question as to whether any disturbance exists or not in any part of the country, this assumption means that the executive can send Federal troops into any community in the United States at his pleasure, and keep them there as long as he chooses. If this is the law, then the principle of self-government either never did exist in this country or else has been destroyed, for no community can be said to possess local self-government, if the executive can, at his pleasure, send military forces to patrol its streets under pretense of enforcing some law. The kind of local self-government that could exist under these circumstances can be found in any of the monarchies of Europe, and it is not in harmony with the spirit of our institutions.

Second—It is also a fundamental principle in our government that except in times of war the military shall be subordinate to the civil authority. In harmony with this provision, the State troops are ordered out to act under and with the civil authorities. The troops you have ordered to Chicago are not under the civil authorities, and are in no way responsible to them for their conduct. They are not even acting under the United States Marshal or any Federal officer of the State, but are acting directly under military orders issued from military headquarters at Washington, and in so far as these troops act at all, it is military government.

Third—The Statute authorizing Federal troops to be sent into States in certain cases contemplates that the State troops shall be taken first. This provision has been ignored and it is assumed that the executive is not bound by it. Federal interference with industrial disturbances in the various States is certainly a new departure, and it opens up so large a field that it will require a very little stretch of authority to absorb to itself all the details of local government.

Fourth—You say that troops were ordered into Illinois upon the demand of the postoffice department, and upon representations of the judicial officers of the United States that process of the courts could not be served, and upon proof that conspiracies existed. We will not discuss the facts, but look for a moment at the principle involved in your statement. All of these officers are appointed by the executive. Most of them can be removed by him at will. They are not only obliged to do his bidding, but they are in fact a part of the executive. If several of them can apply for troops, one alone can; so that under the law, as you assume it to be, an executive, through any one of his appointees, can apply to himself to have the military sent into any city or number of cities, and base his application on such representations as he sees fit to make. In fact, it will be immaterial whether he makes any showing or not, for the executive is the sole judge, and nobody else has any right to interfere or even inquire about it. Then the executive can pass on his own application—his will being the sole guide—he can hold the application to be sufficient, and order troops to as many places as he wishes and put them in command of any one he chooses, and have them act, not under the civil officers, either Federal or State, but directly under military orders from Washington, and there is not in the Constitution or laws, whether written or unwritten, any limitation or restraint upon his power. His judgment, that is, his will, is the sole guide, and it being purely a matter of discretion, his decision can never be examined or questioned.

This assumption as to the power of the executive is certainly new, and I respectfully submit that it is not the law of the land. The jurists have told us that this is a government of law, and not a government by the caprice of an individual, and, further, instead of being autocratic, it is a government of limited power. Yet the autocrat of Russia could certainly not possess, or claim to possess, greater power than is possessed by the executive of the United States, if your assumption is correct.

Fifth—The executive has the command not only of the regular forces of all the United States, but of the military forces of all the States, and can order them to any place he sees fit; and as there are always more or less local disturbances over the country, it will be an easy matter under your construction of the law for an ambitious executive to order out the military forces of all of the States, and establish at once a military government. The only chance of failure in such a movement could come from rebellion, and with such a vast military power at command this could readily be crushed, for, as a rule, soldiers will obey orders.

As for the situation in Illinois, that is of no consequence now compared with the far-reaching principle involved. True, according to my advices, Federal troops have now been on duty for over two days, and although the men were brave and the officers valiant and able, yet their very presence proved to be an irritant because it aroused the indignation of a large class of people, who, while upholding law and order, had been taught to believe in local self-government and, therefore, resented what they regarded as unwarranted interference.

Inasmuch as the Federal troops can do nothing but what the State troops can do there, and believing that the State is amply able to take care of the situation and to enforce the law, and believing that the ordering out of the Federal troops was unwarranted, I again ask their withdrawal.

JOHN P. ALTGELD.

REPUBLICAN PARTY HAS CONDEMNED FEDERAL INTERFERENCE

When all of the facts pertaining to the situation in Chicago are brought out it becomes apparent that if you were to concede the right of the President to send troops to any part of the Union whenever he pleased and on any pretext he pleased, there was no occasion for sending them to Chicago at all and especially not at the time that the order was given, which was in advance of any trouble. Let us consider whether it is true that under our constitution and form of government the Federal government can interfere at will, and for this purpose let us see what construction the Republican party has placed upon the Constitution. It will be remembered that prior to 1861 there was an act of Congress which permitted slave-holders to pursue their slaves through free states and which expressly made it the duty of the courts and all officials to assist the slave-holder in that particular. That act was of the same dignity and had just as much binding force as any other act of Congress could have relating to the exercise of federal power and an order of a federal court made in pursuance of that act would have the same force that an order made under any other act of Congress on this subject would have, and if it is proper to have the United States courts interfere by means of injunction and other orders issued by them to carry out acts of Congress, and if it is proper to use the United States troops to enforce these orders of the United States courts, as is now contended for by the managers of the McKinley campaign, then it was proper for the United States courts prior to 1860 to make such orders and to use the United States troops to enforce those orders. After the Dred Scott decision there were several flagrant cases of federal interference at different places, growing out of this question and when the Republican National Convention met at Chicago in 1860, on the 16th day of May, it adopted a platform which contained the following resolution:

"Section 4. That the maintenance inviolate of the rights of the States, and especially the right of each State to order and control its domestic institutions according to its own judgment exclusively is essential to that balance of power on which the perfection and endurance of our political fabric depends, and we denounce the lawless invasion by armed forces of the soil of any State or Territory, no matter under what pretext, as among the gravest of errors."

The armed forces here referred to were federal forces sent to execute acts of Congress and the orders of federal courts.

THE POLICY OF JEFFERSON

I have not the time to enter upon a general discussion of the principles involved. The Constitution of the United States specified the conditions under which the federal government can interfere in cases of domestic violence in any State. It provides it can be done only on the application of the Legislature or of the State Executive, when the Legislature is not in session. Now, even if it were true, which it is not, that the acts of Congress have attempted to enlarge the powers of the President in this regard, they would be void, because Congress could not, under any pretense, invest the President with any greater power than it has itself under the Constitution. The plank of the Republican platform of 1860, which I have just read, was intended as a condemnation of the use of the federal authority in the affairs of the States under the fugitive slave act of Congress. The old Federalist party, of which the Republican party was the successor, had always leaned toward concentrating power in the federal government, but this plank in the Republican platform followed the doctrines of Jefferson, who said:

"It is by dividing and subdividing these republics from the great national one down through all its subordinations, until it ends in the administration of every man's farm by himself; by placing under every one what his own eye may superintend, that all will be done for the best. What has destroyed liberty and the rights of man in every government which has ever existed under the sun? The generalization and concentrating all cares and powers into one body, no matter whether of the autocrats of Russia or France, or the aristocrats of a Venetian Senate. And I do believe that if the Almighty has not decreed that man shall never be free (and it is a blasphemy to believe it), that the secret will be found to be in the making himself the depository of the powers respecting himself, so far as he is competent to them, and delegating only what is beyond his competence, by a synthetical process, to higher and higher orders of functionaries, so as to trust fewer and fewer powers in proportion as the trustees become more and more remote."

The Democratic National Convention in 1892, in Chicago, which nominated Grover Cleveland for President, contained the following:

"We believe that the public welfare demands that these (Jeffersonian) principles be applied to the conduct of the federal government through the accession to power of the party that advocates them, and we solemnly declare that the need of a return to these fundamental principles of free popular government, based on home rule and individual liberty, was never more urgent than now when the tendency to centralize all power at the federal capital has become a menace to the reserved rights of the States, that strikes at the very roots of our government, under the Constitution as framed by the fathers of the republic."

These are the fundamental principles:

LOCAL SELF-GOVERNMENT THE FOUNDATION OF FREEDOM

The act of the President was an entirely new departure in the history of our government, and Judge Cooley, a great constitutional writer of the country, in complimenting the President upon having taken this step, speaks of it as a great step taken in constitutional construction, and is thankful that it cost so little bloodshed, thus practically stating that this new departure was a violation of the Constitution as it had been understood for a century. The old doctrine of State rights is in no way involved. Nobody for a moment questions the supremacy of the Union. But it does involve the question whether, in connection with federal supremacy, there does not go hand in hand the principle of local self-government. These two principles, i.e., federal union and local self-government, have for a century been regarded as the foundation upon which the glory of our whole governmental fabric rests. One is just as sacred, just as inviolable, just as important as the other. Without federal union there must follow anarchy, and without local self-government there must follow despotism. Both are destructive, not only of the liberties, but of the higher aspirations and possibilities of a people. The great Civil War settled that we should not have anarchy. It remains to be settled whether we shall be destroyed by despotism. If the President can, at his pleasure, in the first instance, send troops into any city, town or hamlet in the country, or into any number of cities, towns or hamlets in the country, whenever and wherever he pleases (as is now contended he can) under the pretense of enforcing some act of Congress, his judgment, which means his pleasure, being the sole criterion, then there can be no difference whatever in this respect between the powers of the President and those of Emperor William or of the Czar of Russia. Neither of these potentates ever claimed anything more. The question is whether the local and State authorities should not first be called to enforce the law and maintain order, using for that purpose such local agencies and forces as the law has created, or whether he can ignore all these and bring a foreign force and station it in any community at pleasure. In this respect federal civil officers and the federal army do not stand on the same footing. The federal civil officers always have acted directly in the matter within their jurisdiction, but the American people, as all other free and intelligent people, are jealous of a central military power, hence great precautions have been taken to limit the use of such power, and these limitations have always been recognized in this country, and were recognized by the Attorney General so late as June 16, 1894. Again, the Constitution provides that the military shall be subordinate to the civil authorities, and in all cases where State troops are ordered out they are subject to the control of the local civil authorities and act under their direction, but the federal troops ordered to Chicago in 1894 did not act under any civil officer, whether federal or State. They did not act under the United States Marshal, but directly under orders from military headquarters at Washington, and were subject to those orders only. So far as they acted at all, it was military government. Local self-government is the very foundation of freedom and of republican institutions, and no people possess this who are subject to have the army patrol their streets, acting not under, but independently of the local authorities, and do this at the mere discretion of one man, or of a central power that is far away. Such local self-government as would be possible under these conditions may be found all over Russia. We grew great and powerful and won the admiration of the world while proceeding under a different form of government, and if we are to go on in this same line, then the American people must arrest and rebuke this federal usurpation. In all history no power possessed by government was ever allowed to lie dormant long. Either the man or the class soon appeared who, for selfish purposes, proceeded to exercise it. If the acts of the President are to stand unchallenged and thus form a precedent, then we have undergone a complete change in our form of government, and whatever semblance we may keep up in the future, our career as a republic is over. We will have a rapidly increasing central power controlled and dominated by class and by corporate interests. Holding these views and knowing that the law had been enforced, property protected and order maintained for a whole century by constitutional agencies, and feeling that the mighty State of Illinois needed neither assistance nor interference from any outside source, I considered it my duty, as the executive of the State, to protest against the presence of federal troops under the existing circumstances, and requested their withdrawal. It is a matter of special regret to many of our patriotic citizens that this blow at free institutions should have been struck by a President who was placed in power by a party that had made local self-government a cardinal principle for more than a century.

According to Judge Cooley, Mr. Cleveland gave the Constitution a new construction. This may be true, but he stabbed republican government to the vitals when he did it.

I have felt disposed to excuse ex-Mayor Hopkins on the ground that it was natural for him to want his administration to demonstrate its ability to do what prior administrations had done. But, however this may be, he is now working for the election of McKinley by trying to defeat the Democratic candidate. Let the McKinley orators abuse him if they like.

In the fall of 1874, during the administration of President Grant, the governor of Louisiana applied for federal troops to quell internal disturbances in that State, and acting on this request troops were sent there. On January 4, 1875, by order of the governor, these troops dispersed the lower house of the Legislature on the ground that it was a mere mob, and the action of the troops was sustained and endorsed by the administration at Washington. This aroused indignation throughout the Northern States, and on January 15, 1875, a meeting was held in Faneuil Hall, Boston, to protest against this act of the federal government. Mr. William Gray was made President and there was a large list list of Vice-Presidents, comprising a number of the most distinguished men of Boston.

At this meeting resolutions were adopted which strongly condemned the administration—Mr. Gray, Col. Henry Lee, Gen. S. M. Quincy, John Quincy Adams, Hon. F. W. Bird, Hon. Leverett Saltonstall, Hon. Albert Mason, Richard Olney and Robert M. Morse made speeches. Mr. Olney among other things said: "Apparently the administration meant to assert that the President might enter a State with troops to suppress disorder and violence at his own discretion upon his own view of the exigency and without waiting for the request or consent of the State itself. No more glaring attempt at usurpation can be imagined. If successful it would revolutionize our whole governmental system and clearly annihiliate the right of local self government by a State.

Mr. Olney here struck the right key note, and as shown by his dispatch to Judge Allen at Springfield, he still held this view on June 16, 1894. It was immediately after this last date that the great corporations demanded that a new precedent be set and that the federal government take them directly under its wing so that they might ignore and in the end defy local government. As Mr. Olney was himself a corporation man he joined with Mr. Cleveland in granting this demand. Attempts have been made to draw a distinction between the laws of Congress and the United States courts on the one hand and the laws of a State and State tribunals on the other, claiming that federal troops could be used in the first instance to execute the laws of Congress and the decrees of the United States courts while the State troops could be used only to execute the laws of the State and the processes of State tribunals. But there is no such distinction, nor was there ever before such a contention.

The laws of Congress are the laws of each State and of each city just as much as the acts of the State legislature or of a city council. And it is the duty of a State and of a city to execute and enforce the laws of Congress just as much as it is to enforce the local laws. In this respect there is no distinction between laws. The mere fact that the federal government as a matter of expediency has seen fit to create judicial machinery to enforce the laws of the United States does not relieve a State nor even a city of the fundamental duty of enforcing the laws of the United States. To repeat—these laws are just as much in force as the acts of the State legislature or the ordinances of a city government.

Local self government means that a municipality or a state shall use all the power in its possession to enforce all laws that are in force within its borders whether they be federal, State or municipal, and if the powers of the State is inadequate for this purpose then the Constitution has provided a method for bringing in federal troops.

It is as much the duty of the State to furnish all necessary force to execute the process of a federal court held within its borders as it is to furnish the necessary force to execute the process of a State tribunal. Mr. Olney clearly recognized this principle when he telegraphed Judge Allen of the United States court at Springfield that the United States marshal of that district should apply to the State for the necessary assistance to execute the process and the decrees of the United States courts.

To further illustrate this point: the fugitive slave law was an act of Congress—it was a law of the United States. The United States courts in a number of instances rendered judgments and decrees under this law and it was to execute these judgments and decrees that the United States forces were sent to assist the United States marshal at Boston and in several other instances prior to 1860. As already shown, when the national Republican convention met in Chicago in 1860 it violently denounced these acts of federal interference, as destructive of our institutions, and Mr. Lincoln denounced these acts with great earnestness in his speeches. The fact that the federal troops had been used to execute decrees of the United States courts founded on acts of Congress was not accepted as a justification.

It has been asked: "Suppose the officials and the people of a State in time of trouble refuse to enforce the law and refuse to ask for federal assistance, then must you let all society go to destruction?" You might as well ask, "Suppose the President failed or refused to do his duty then would the republic perish and all society be destroyed?"

This idea is absurd and grows out of the assumption that we exist and are held together by a force coming from above, instead of governing ourselves. It assumes that seventy millions of people may go to destruction and free institutions be destroyed unless some official reaches out and saves them. It ignores the fact that our government is founded on the theory that the people themselves do the governing and that the world's experience has shown that they can be trusted a thousand times over rather than some office-holder, and it further ignores the fact that for one hundred and twenty years the people of this country have so governed themselves, and that it was during this time that our institutions were developed, our cities were built and our greatness was achieved.

AMATEUR SAVIORS OF SOCIETY

It is amazing to see the young saviors of society that have recently sprung up. During the one hundred and twenty years in which this country grew great and won the admiration of the world they were unheard of and were not needed. But through the accident of an election or an appointment they were brought to the attention of the American people and then these debutants suddenly felt that the responsibility of saving the republic was on them and that society would go to destruction unless they reached out and saved it. All the intelligence, the ability, the patriotism, yea, the experience and success in self government counts for naught, and we have been given to understand that unless a few young men, some of whom had borrowed money to get a new suit of clothes before going to Washington, now save society, all will be lost.

GOVERNMENT BY INJUNCTION

The immortal Jefferson, after having written the Declaration of Independence and helped to launch the new republic, watched the operations of the new government for years, and with a vision that was prophetic wrote the following:

"It has long been my opinion and I have never shrunk from its expression, that the germ of dissolution of our federal government is in the constitution of the federal judiciary, an irresponsible body working like gravity, by day and by night, gaining a little to-day and a little to-morrow and advancing its noiseless step like a thief over the field of jurisdiction until all shall be usurped from the States and the government of all become consolidated into one. To this I am opposed because when all government, domestic and foreign, in little and in great things shall be drawn to Washington as the center of all power, it will render powerless the checks provided of one government on another and will become as venal and oppressive as the government from which we separated."

See how accurately he located the danger and described the future. I have not the time to point out the alarming encroachments and usurpations of the federal courts since the days of Jefferson. I will only call attention to their most recent and astounding pretension and usurpation of power. During the last decade they have established a form of government that is government by injunction, under which the federal judge becomes at once legislator, judge and executioner. Sitting in his chambers and without notice to anybody he issues a ukase, which he calls an injunction, against all the people of a State, forbidding anything that he sees fit to forbid and which the law does not forbid, for when the law forbids a thing there is no need of an injunction. When the law is violated provision has been made for punishment, and if it is found at any time to be inadequate it can always be remedied by legislation. But by this injunction the judge can forbid anything which whim, prejudice or caprice may suggest, and his order is law and must stand until it is reversed by a superior authority, and this may take months and even years, and when any individual disregards this injunction he is arrested by the United States marshal and dragged to the point where the court is held, sometimes a distance of a hundred or a hundred and fifty miles, away from his friends, on a charge, not of committing a crime, not of violating the law, but on a charge of being guilty of contempt of court, that is, of having disregarded the judge's injunction, and he is tried, not by a jury, as guaranteed by the Constitution and laws of the land, not according to the forms of law even, but he is tried by the same judge whose dignity he is charged with having offended, and then he is sent to prison indefinitely. Had he committed a murder or a heinous crime, had he violated the law in a flagrant manner he would have been entitled to be tried by a jury, according to the forms of law, and in the county where the offense was committed and where he could produce his witnesses, but not so when he is guilty of showing a want of respect for the order of a judge which was made outside of the law and in violation of the Constitution. When the Sultan of Turkey or the Czar of Russia issues a ukase forbidding something that the law had not forbidden he at least leaves the task of trying those who are charged with disregarding this ukase to some other individual. Common decency and common justice would suggest such a course, but in our country a federal judge assumes to do things which would be discountenanced even in Russia or Turkey. Several years ago it was charged that the management of the Northern Pacific railway had robbed that road of about sixty million dollars, and after this charge was made the same managers went before Judge Jenkins, of the United States court at Milwaukee, and got him to appoint their friend, Mr. Henry C. Payne of Milwaukee, and two other friends, as receivers of the road, and instead of trying to collect back the sums that were charged to have been wrongfully taken from the road the first thing that Mr. Payne did was to reduce the wages of the men who worked on the road, and did it without notice to the men, and then he, together with his attorney, Mr. Spooner of Wisconsin, went before this same Judge Jenkins and he got that judge to issue an injunction forbidding the men from quitting the employment of the road. This also was issued without notice to the men. If any man quit the employment of the road while that injunction was in force he was guilty of contempt of court, liable to be tried, not by a jury, but by the judge who issued the injunction himself, and sent to prison indefinitely. A somewhat similar order to this had been made some time previous by a federal judge at Toledo, Ohio.

Judge Ross of California issued an injunction compelling the employes of a railroad to go to work. Think of a judge legislating that way. When an individual has an employe who won't work he discharges him, but this judge ordered railroad employes sent to jail if they did not go to work. He undertook to run a railroad and just sat down and made law to suit him. He legislated, judged and executed. The Constitution, the law, trial by jury, and the rights of the citizen were all brushed aside by this federal judge. During the railroad strike of 1894 Judges Wood and Grosscup, in the United States court at Chicago, issued a number of these injunctions which, in so far as they forbade what the law forbade were unnecessary, and in so far as they forbade what the law did not forbid amounted to new legislation. After they were issued the farce was enacted of having an officer attempt to read them to a mob, which, under the circumstances, could neither hear nor understand them, and the United States marshal at Chicago swore in four thousand, four hundred and two deputy marshals for the purpose of enforcing these injunctions. Some of these injunctions were obtained as early as June 29 and June 30, a number of days ahead of any trouble, yet as a preventative they were total failures and accomplished nothing. The trouble kept spreading and growing just as if there had been no injunctions. According to their own statements the United States marshals arrested about four hundred and fifty men on a mere charge of being guilty of a contempt of court, and these had nearly all to be discharged after having been dragged to the court because nothing whatever could be proved against them. One man was a train master and had done nothing whatever except simply to quit work, but he had won the enmity of his superior and he was arrested, was taken a hundred miles in charge of officers, remained in their custody for several days, and when his case came to be heard he was dismissed with the simple statement that the government did not care to prosecute. For the time the corporations, through Mr. Walker, were the government. In other cases men were taken a hundred and a hundred and fifty miles from their homes and were lodged in jail until their cases could be heard and had to be discharged because nothing could be proved against them and then they found themselves penniless and had to beg their way back. Through these injunctions certain corporations and individuals have been able, at various times, to make a kind of side door convenience of the federal courts and thus lower and destroy the respect for and confidence in the tribunals of justice and create the impression in the land that courts, by making law for themselves and robbing men of a trial by jury and violating the Constitution, are instruments of oppression.

GOVERNMENT BY INJUNCTION A USURPATION

A mere glance at this invasion shows that government by injunction is incompatible with republican institutions, and if it is to be sustained then there is an end to trial by jury in our country, and instead of being governed by law we will be subject to government by judges, and if government by injunction is to be sustained as to federal judges, then we will soon have it on the part of State judges and the very foundations of free institutions will have disappeared. These injunctions are outside of the regular machinery of government; so far as they are outside of the law they are usurpations, and where they are not usurpations, they are wrong, because the Constitution has created other machinery to enforce the criminal law. Courts of chancery were not created for this purpose. In Chicago they did not prevent the burning of a freight car or the ditching of a train. Our country has existed for more than a hundred years. During this time all our greatness and our glory has been achieved. Property has been protected, law and order has been maintained by the machinery established by the Constitution. This machinery has at all times been found to be sufficient for every emergency. If both the Constitution and our past experience are now to be disregarded and the courts are to be permitted to set up this new form of government, then the affairs of life will soon be regulated, not by law, but by the personal pleasure, prejudice or caprice of a multitude of judges. Formerly, when a man charged with contempt filed an affidavit purging himself of the contempt, that is, denying it, the matter ended. All that could be done was to prosecute him for perjury if he had sworn to what was not true. But after thus purging himself he could not be tried for contempt by the very judge whose dignity he was charged with having offended. In other words, when a man denied his guilt he could not be sentenced to prison without a trial by jury. But this protection of the citizen is now brushed away with a mere wave of the hand. The citizen is robbed of a trial by jury, and he is tried by the judge for whom he is alleged to have shown a want of respect and is sent to prison indefinitely.

It was the extraordinary action of a few judges that called the attention of the American people to the possibilities and to the extremely dangerous character of this system, and which makes law abiding and patriotic men feel that if not checked it must destroy free institutions.

THE SUPREME COURT

The Chicago platform denounces the peculiar conduct of the Supreme Court in the income tax case.

The platform declares that the income tax law had been passed in strict pursuance of the uniform decisions of that court for nearly one hundred years; that the court had in the last decision sustained objections to that law which had previously been over-ruled by the same court, and the platform therefore in substance declares in favor of securing the reversal of that decision if possible and of having Congress do all in its power to equalize the burdens of taxation so that wealth may bear its due propor-tion of the expense of government.

This criticism of the Supreme Court is denounced as subver-sive of order and destructive of the respect that is due that tribunal. Astonishing as it may appear, men formerly connected with the Democratic party and men connected with the Repub-lican party insist that courts are of a sacred character and above the reach of criticism. My friends, I give way to no man in ad-miration for American institutions. My life has been spent in trying to protect the flag of my country and trying to advance the educational institutions of the country, and as an officer of the court serving in the capacity of prosecutor and for five years as a judge of the superior court of Chicago, and after this ex-perience at the bar and on the bench, I say to my countrymen that there cannot be in a republic any institution exempt from criticism, and that when any institute is permitted to assume that attitude it will destroy republican government. The judicial branch of the government is just as much subject to the criticism of the American people as are the legislative or executive branches, and it needs this criticism more than does either of the other two branches, because by reason of frequent changes the people can make their will felt in the legislative and executive offices, but as the federal judges are not appointed by the people and are not responsible to them, and for all practical purposes cannot be reached except by the moral sentiment and sense of justice created in the public mind by free criticism. The judges of our federal courts are as honest as other men and no more so. They have the same passions and prejudices that other men have, and are just as liable to make mistakes and to move in the wrong direction as other men are, and the safety of the republic not only permits, but actually requires, that the action of the courts should be honestly and thoroughly scanned and be freely criticised, not with a view of arousing resistance to the decision of the court, but for the purpose of forcing the court in the end to see its error and to correct it. The mere fact that the Supreme Court has all through its career repeatedly reversed its own decisions shows its fallibility. Everybody admits that the decision of a court is binding in the case in which it was rendered and until it is reversed constitutes a precedent to indicate how the courts will decide the same question again, but this fact does not prevent men from doing what they can to get the court to reverse its decision. Nor does the decision of the Supreme Court in any case become a rule of political action the correctness of which the voter dare not question. The Supreme Court cannot by mere decision upon a constitutional question rob the people of the powers of self-government nor prevent the American people from deciding for themselves, through the properly constituted machinery, whether they will accept the decision of the Supreme Court as being final or whether they will refuse to accept it as a rule of action. As Mr. Lincoln said, "It does not necessarily become a rule of political action." The people have not parted with their power of self-government in favor of either legislative, executive or the judicial branch of the government. For the benefit of so-called Democrats who have criticised this plank in the platform, I would recall the language of Jefferson already quoted, and will add the following: In 1800 Mr. Jefferson wrote to a friend as follows: "You seem to consider the judges as the ultimate arbiters of all constitutional questions. A very dangerous doctrine indeed and one which would place us under the despotism of an oligarchy. Our judges are as honest as other men and not more so. They have with others the same passions for party, for power, and the privilege of their corps and their power is the more dangerous, as they are in office for life and not responsible as the other functionaries are to the elective control. The Constitution has erected no such tribunal, knowing that to whatever hands confided with the corruption of time and of party its members would become despots. The Constitution has more wisely made all the departments co-equal and co-sovereign within themselves." I would likewise remind you of the language of Andrew Jackson. After the Supreme Court had held the national bank bill to be constitutional in all parts, he refused to be bound by that decision, and asserted that he, as President, would not be bound to hold the national bank to be constitutional, even though the Supreme Court had decided it to be so. He accepted the doctrine of Mr. Jefferson and acted upon it under his official oath in vetoing a charter for the national bank, and I would remind the Republicans who are making this criticism of the attitude of Lincoln toward the Supreme Court when discussing the Dred Scott decision in the Lincoln and Douglas debate, when in referring to that decision he said: "We do oppose that decision as a political rule which shall be binding on a voter to vote for nobody who thinks it wrong; which shall be binding on the members of Congress or the President to favor no measure that does not actually concur with the principles of that decision. We do not propose to be bound by it as a political rule in that way. Judge Douglas would make that decision a rule of political action for the people and all of the departments of the government. I would not. By resisting it as a political rule, I disturb no right of property, create no disorder and incite no mobs." Again he says, "We offer no resistance to the Dred Scott decision, but we think it is erroneous. We know the court that made it has often overruled its own decisions, and we shall do what we can to have it overrule this one."

In his first inaugural address he said: "The candid citizen must confess that if the policy of the government, upon vital questions affecting the whole people, is to be irrevocably fixed by decisions of the Supreme Court, the instant they are made, as in ordinary litigation between parties in personal actions, the people will have ceased to be their own rulers, having to that extent practically resigned their government into the hands of that eminent tribunal."

CHICAGO PLATFORM VOICES JEFFERSONIAN DOCTRINE

Now that is the attitude which the Chicago platform takes toward the Supreme Court at present. It recognizes the decision of the court as being binding so long as it stands, but we believe the decision to be wrong and in violation of the Constitution. It was made by a divided court and under circumstances that look very strange, if not suspicious, to the American people.

Let me quote a little more standard Republican authority. Senator Sumner, on the floor of the Senate on February 3, 1865, in referring to the Dred Scott decision, charged Chief Justice Taney with flagrantly perverting the truth of history. He compared him with the infamous Jeffreys of England, charged him with being a tool of the slave power, and said: "I declare that the opinion of the Chief Justice in the case of Dred Scott was more thoroughly abominable than anything of the kind in the history of courts. Then and there judicial baseness reached its lowest points. An outrageous judgment was sustained by falsification of history; the Constitution of the United States, every principle of liberty and historical truth were falsified."

But we need not look for authority outside of the court itself upon the question as to whether it is sacred or is exceedingly fallible and needs the wholesome influence of criticism as well as any other institution in this country. Let me read you a few sentences from the dissenting opinion in the income tax case of Mr. Justice White, concurred in by Justice Harlan, both members of that court: "I consider that the result of the opinion of the court just announced is to overthrow a long and consistent line of decisions and to deny to the legislative department of the government the possession of a power conceded to it by universal consensus for one hundred years, and which has been recognized by repeated adjudications of this court." And again he says: "And now after one hundred years, after long continued action by other departments of the government, and after repeated adjudications by this court, this interpretation is overthrown, and the Congress is declared not to have a power of taxation which may at some time, as it has in the past, prove necessary to the very existence of the government."

And again: "Great as is my respect for any view announced by this court, I cannot resist the conviction that its opinion in this case annuls its previous decisions in regard to the powers of Congress on the subject of taxation, and is therefore fraught with danger to the court, to each and every citizen and to the republic. The conservative and orderly development of our institutions rest on our acceptance of the results of the past. Their use as lights guide our steps in the future. Teach the lesson that settled principles may be overthrown at any time and confusion and turmoil must ultimately result."

SUPREME COURT NOT INFALLIBLE

Now, my fellow citizens, we insist that the language in this Chicago platform relating to the Supreme Court is more kindly and is much more respectful than was the language of any of the great men I have named. These great men all recognized the fact that that court, like all other courts, is fallible, as all other human institutions are. That while its decisions were binding and conclusive in the cases in which they were rendered and were entitled to great respect in all cases, yet to accept them as a binding rule of political action would lead to the destruction of republican institutions and the establishment in the end of oligarchy in government. And when you reflect that we have already reached a point where a federal judge, in fact, several federal judges, have actually issued orders prohibiting men who are working for a railroad from quitting their employment and threatened to imprison men for refusing to work, you see that there is no limit to the authority which they attempt to exercise.

For a number of years the great corporations and trusts and syndicates have carefully looked after the matter of appointments to the federal bench, and so great was their influence that few could be appointed who were not satisfactory to them. In many cases men were taken out of the corporation offices and put on the federal bench. These men brought with them all of the bias and prejudice that take possession of men who have long been subject to corporate influence and environment, and when some of these men trample justice and equity under foot and render outrageous decisions in the interest of their former employers, shall it be said that the American people have no right to criticise their action just as they would criticise the action of a governor or a legislature? If they have not this right when did they lose it? Let me remind you, my countrymen, that neither the poor people nor the great toiling masses of the earth have ever destroyed a government. All the great governments and institutions of the past were destroyed by the rich and powerful, who shut their eyes to injustice and, through selfish greed, inaugurated policies that pulled down the pillars of state, and while thus engaged in bringing ruin upon their country they made a pharisaical pretense of patriotism. These things are now happening in our land.

QUESTIONS INVOLVED

No campaign ever made in this country involved so many far-reaching questions as this one does. Questions, every one of which goes to the foundation of free government and affects the perpetuity of our institutions.

First—The question whether the people have surrendered the right of self-government into the hands of the Supreme Court of the United States, and whether the courts are thus placed above criticism and their acts exempt from that scrutiny which every patriotic and intelligent man should give to the acts of the other branches of the government.

Second—Whether both the constitution and the traditions of the government shall henceforth be ignored and the President shall be conceded the power of sending federal troops at his pleasure into any neighborhood in the United States or a thousand neighborhoods at one time; troops who will not be subject to the civil authorities nor to the local authorities; who are under instructions from Washington; whether this can be done not only without the request of the local authorities, but in defiance of them?

Third—Whether the people of this country and especially the laboring masses who do not have much of a voice in the selection of judges shall recognize and thus perpetuate the system of governing by injunction, which does away with constitutional government, which does away with government by law, does away with trial by jury, does away with trial according to the forms of law and substitutes the caprice, whim, prejudice or passion of a judge for all these, making him at once legislator, judge and to a certain extent executioner?

Fourth—Whether we shall dissolve in boodle, bribery and corruption. Whether the men who have grown great as lobbyists shall rule this land. Whether we shall declare to the world scoundrelism is in the end the loftiest form of patriotism. It is a remarkable fact that those men and those influences whose slime is dissolving our institutions are all helping Mr. Hanna. Everything within their reach is being prostituted. Where they can, they degrade the religious press and defile the pulpit. They have dragged the American flag in the mire by using it as an advertising sheet for McKinley and Hobart. In Chicago it is a fitting coincidence that most of the buildings from which the flag is thus degraded do not pay their fair share of taxes. Wave the flag and plunder the public, is the gospel of McKinleyism.

Fifth—Whether the British monetary policy shall be made perpetual so that the toiling and producing masses of this country will be reduced in their purchasing power; will be reduced in the end to a lower plane of civilization; will be reduced in the end to the conditions of the men who till the fields of Europe or the Valley of the Nile?

McKINLEY VS. THE PEOPLE

It is a remarkable circumstance that Mark Hanna and the whole crowd of men who are supporting this British policy of plutocracy are against the people of this country on all of these great questions. That crowd of men who nominated Mr. McKinley and who treat him as a kind of convenience, favor federal military interference, sustain the usurpation of the federal courts, sustain government by injunction, and sustain this English monetary policy which makes everything that the American people produce, everything that the American people create, cheap, while it makes what the English have to sell, namely, money, very dear.

The American people are called on this year to make a new declaration of independence to mankind. Over a hundred years ago the declaration that was made by less than three million people to the world was that they were not only free but that they were independent of all the nations of the earth; now the American people are asked to announce to the world that free institutions have perished among them; that the President of the United States has arbitrary power with respect to the use of troops, as great as the Czar of Russia or Emperor William; they are asked to announce to the world that the people have given up and surrendered to the courts of the United States the power of self-government and are bound now to take without question or without criticism whatever policy those courts may dictate; the people are asked to make a declaration to the world that we are no longer governed absolutely by law and according to the forms of law, but that the right of trial by jury has been abolished and that every man now walks the streets only by the grace of the federal courts. We are asked to make a declaration to mankind that we were once free and were once independent of all the nations on the globe, but we are now a mere financial dependency of England. These are the issues involved in this campaign. Low prices have destroyed the purchasing power of our farmers and in that way have shut up the mills and the factories, turned the laborer out of his job because there was and is no market for what he makes. Low prices have spread poverty, misery and increased crime throughout the civilized world. They are the result of that legislation in Europe and in this country which interfered with the law of supply and demand with regard to money; that legislation which by destroying a part of the world's supply of money and by making gold the sole standard increased the demand for gold. So long as this standard is perpetuated so long will these conditions, which it has produced, continue. If the toiling masses of this country, if the patriotic men of this country favor a continuation of these conditions then let them vote for Mr. Hanna and plutocracy, for Mr. McKinley is scarcely a factor in this campaign. Mr. Mark Hanna and the agents of syndicates and trusts constitute the power that is subverting free institutions.

A NEW DECLARATION OF INDEPENDENCE

My fellow citizens, if you do not believe in the policy advocated by these men, if you are not in favor of converting this republic into an oligarchy, if you believe that this country should at least be in part governed by the men who toil and not solely and alone governed by the men who devour the fruit that others toil for, then rise in your manhood, stand out in the sun and before the Almighty declare, as did the fathers over a hundred years ago, that we are not only a free but that we are an independent people. Declare that the time has not yet come when this country must be made a financial dependency upon England, that the experiment of twenty odd years of having the world's business done on a single gold standard has been a failure, that it has covered the earth with misery and distress, and that it must be brought to an end. Stand up and declare that this country must return to that standard of prices which had been the world's standard through all the countries that have passed; that standard under which the foundations of this republic were laid, under which we grew great and mighty and became the most powerful people of the earth; that standard under which everything that is great, grand and glorious in the world today was created; that standard upon which this wonderful civilization of the nineteenth century rests. Declare yourselves to be in favor of that policy under which the mints shall again be opened to both of the metals so that there will be an end of this destructive fall in prices; so that prudent men will again feel that it is safe to go into business or to embark in new enterprises. Declare in favor of an American policy which will result in instantly inducing intelligent and enterprising men to open up new fields of industry, which will at once create a demand for all kinds of labor, all kinds of skill and for all kinds of talents. Our fathers made a declaration of independence and there followed a century of the grandest development ever known upon the earth. If you believe in the institutions of the fathers and in perpetuating them, then go to the polls on the 3d of November and make a new declaration of independence and there will follow another century which in grandeur and glory and in achievement and the blessings to be showered upon mankind will surpass the century that is closing.

RETIRING ADDRESS AS GOVERNOR OF ILLINOIS

Prepared for delivery at Springfield, January 11, 1897

Vilified, ill, exhausted, and virtually bankrupt, his health and his fortune spent, Governor Altgeld failed in his bid for re-election.

According to custom, he prepared an address to be delivered at the inauguration of the incoming governor. But the campaign of insult and defamation carried on against Altgeld was to follow him to the very end of his career as a public official, and, on the day of the inaugural ceremony, Altgeld's successor—casting aside both custom and courtesy—refused to permit him to speak. Altgeld's farewell address, although never delivered, reached the public through newspaper publication of the text.

This occasion does not invite extended remarks from me. The world has decreed that an actor who has played his part shall simply make his bow and retire from the stage. Men turn their faces toward the rising sun and so it should be, for while the past may admonish it is the future that inspires.

But we may pause long enough to note the character of this occasion and the lesson it teaches. It took the world thousands of years to reach a point where such a scene as this was possible. Mankind struggled through weary and bloody centuries before anything like government was evolved and then there followed dark ages before it became possible to take the reins of government out of the hands of one political party and place them in the hands of a hostile party without blood-shed. The scene which we witness here to-day shows the triumph of republican government and teaches us that the journey of man, when viewed from headland to headland, has been onward and upward; that passion is retiring and reason is mounting the throne, and we may congratulate ourselves upon the fact that in this great advancement America has set the example for the nations.

The presence of the defeated and retiring party is not necessary for the peaceful change of administration, yet in order to add the graces to republican form it is customary for the retiring party to be represented and participate in the ceremonies of inauguration, and to-day the great party which I have the honor to represent, not only assists in these ceremonies, but it expresses the hope that the new administration will direct the destinies of this mighty State along the paths of honor and of glory. While politically divided we are all Illinoisans and the greatness and the grandeur of this State rise above all considerations of persons or of party. Her past thrills, her present awes and her future dazzles the intellect of man.

To the distinguished gentleman who is to stand at her head I extend the most cordial greeting and hearty good wishes. Loving Illinois as I do I shall applaud his every act that tends to her advancement. I have given her four of my best years and have brought all my offerings to her altar. Had it been necessary to do so I should have considered life itself but a small sacrifice in her interest and I retire from her service and from the high office to which her people elected me without any trace of bitterness or disappointment. I have tried to further the best interests of my country, and while I erred in many cases they were errors of judgment and I go forth with a peaceful conscience. I have endeavored to carry out those principles that form the basis of free government and I have acted on the conviction that it would be better to be Governor but for one day and follow the dictates of justice than to hold office for fifty years by winking at wrong. In my judgment no epitaph can be written upon the tomb of a public man that will so surely win the contempt of the ages than to say of him that he held office all his life and never did anything for humanity. We believe that the institutions of the State are in excellent condition. Some of my friends feel that we have been cleaning house; that we have been putting things in order. Permit me to say that if any of the measures which we have inaugurated should prove beneficial to the country the people will be in no wise indebted to me, for when a public man gives to his country the very best services in his power he has done no more than he agreed to do and has done no more than the public had a right to expect. I do not endorse the charge that republics are ungrateful. I believe that in the end there is a disposition to give every man his meed. In fact, many men have been loaded by republics with honors which were far beyond their deserts. We turn the affairs of the State over to our successors.

I would remind my distinguished successor that there is no such thing as repose in the universe; that the centripetal and centrifugal laws are constantly at work; that nothing stands still; that nothing is ever perfect; that there is a perpetual development and a constant disintegration, and that the institutions of this State must go on developing, reaching a higher and a higher plane successively, or they must retrograde, and I will further say to him that rarely does the hand of fate open the gate to a more alluring pathway of glory than is open to him now. Illinois is already the guiding star of the American constellation. Her people have outstripped all other peoples of the earth and they will surely shape the destiny of this republic. Their institutions of every kind and character should be the models for the earth and the flame of intelligence burning on her prairies and by the inland sea must brighten the sky for all people, and there could not possibly be a greater achievement than to assist in directing the thought and shaping the institutions of such a people.

But I warn my distinguished friend and successor that the task is not a light one. It is beset with the greatest difficulties and will require wisdom, courage and intense determination and persistence. The selfish forces of greed are always ready to tear to pieces the noblest creations of patriotism. Hence it has been well said that the tablets of immortality are harder than flint and that only persevering genius can engrave a name or an act there.

To the members of that great political party to which I have the honor of belonging let me say that while we are relieved of the responsibility of administration our responsibility in another direction is increased, for in a republic it is the minority party which creates the sentiment and develops the principles which the government shall in the end carry out. Not being hampered or embarrassed by the detail of administration, the minority party can devote its best energies to the discussion of great principles, while the majority party, being obliged to conciliate conflicting interests and to compromise, is in that respect hampered and generally spends its force in endeavoring to carry out a policy already determined upon by the country and is not able to deal in an independent manner with new questions which are from time to time evolved. It is the minority party that has made progress possible not only in this country but in Europe. In England it was the minority party that repeatedly forced the government to adopt new and great reforms. The immortal orators of England spoke for the minority. In our country the great forensic efforts which helped to move the nation forward were made by men who stood in the ranks of the minority. In fact, every great reform in our country had to first confront a hostile majority. In a sense the mission of the minority is of a higher order than that of the majority. True, it does not deal in spoils, it has no fleshpots to distribute, but it is its high mission to discover the eternal essence of things and to point out the way of justice.

We go out of power with nothing to regret. Conscious of having struggled for a great cause we smile at the frowns of fate and go forth with renewed hope and a firmer purpose. We need not inquire what were the reasons for our defeat. We know there were some conditions for which we were not responsible, and on account of these conditions the currents began to run against us nearly three years ago and they ran with such irresistible force two years ago that they covered the State like a deluge, submerging everything. In the last campaign the same currents were still running with the same force, other hostile forces were added which in themselves seemed irresistible. Our party was obliged to reform as it were in the face of the enemy. It eliminated many elements of weakness, elements which for years had tended to neutralize the party and make it impotent, so that it stood for no definite or great principle and was incapable of making an aggressive fight. After eliminating these elements of weakness the party made one of the grandest campaigns ever witnessed.

But all this belongs to the past. No American has a right to stand with his face toward that which is gone. Government is the constant meeting of new conditions. It is not the things of yesterday but the things of to-morrow that must engage our attention. The principles we hold are the only ones upon which free government can endure. Let us renew our devotion to them and kindle anew our enthusiasm. Let us not follow the example of those who try to use the names of Jefferson and Jackson to hide the most undemocratic principles and even the most destructive practices. In so far as the new administration, federal and State, shall adhere to the great doctrines of human right and shall adhere to those great principles that lie at the very basis of republican institutions let us give them our hearty commendation and support, but let us be watchful and whenever it shall seem to us that the welfare and prosperity of our great country are being endangered let us raise the alarm and let us all the time feel an abiding confidence that right will in the end prevail.

EPILOGUE—"JOHN PETER ALTGELD, 1847-1902"

Memorial address by Clarence Darrow, delivered at Chicago, April 20, 1902

In the Great Flood of human life that is spawned upon the earth, it is not often that a man is born. The friend and comrade that we mourn today was formed of that infinitely rare mixture that now and then at long, long intervals combines to make a man. John P. Altgeld was one of the rarest souls who ever lived and died. His was a humble birth, a fearless life and a dramatic, fitting death. We who knew him, we who loved him, we who rallied to his many hopeless calls, we who dared to praise him while his heart still beat, cannot yet feel that we shall never hear his voice again.

John P. Altgeld was a soldier tried and true; not a soldier clad in uniform, decked with spangles and led by fife and drum in the mad intoxication of the battlefield; such soldiers have not been rare upon the earth in any land or age. John P. Altgeld was a soldier in the everlasting struggle of the human race for liberty and justice on the earth. From the first awakening of his young mind until the last relentless summons came, he was a soldier who had no rest or furlough, who was ever on the field in the forefront of the deadliest and most hopeless fight, whom none but death could muster out. Liberty, the relentless goddess, had turned her fateful smile on John P. Altgeld's face when he was but a child, and to this first, fond love he was faithful unto death.

Liberty is the most jealous and exacting mistress that can beguile the brain and soul of man. She will have nothing from him who will not give her all. She knows that his pretended love serves but to betray. But when once the fierce heat of her quench-less, lustrous eyes has burned into the victim's heart, he will know no other smile but hers. Liberty will have none but the great devoted souls, and by her glorious visions, her lavish prom-ises, her boundless hopes, her infinitely witching charms, she lures her victims over hard and stony ways, by desolate and dangerous paths, through misery, obloquy and want to a martyr's cruel death. Today we pay our last sad homage to the most de-voted lover, the most abject slave, the fondest, wildest, dream-iest victim that ever gave his life to liberty's immortal cause.

In the history of the country where he lived and died, the life and works of our devoted dead will one day shine in words of everlasting light. When the bitter feelings of the hour have passed away, when the mad and poisonous fever of commercial-ism shall have run its course, when conscience and honor and justice and liberty shall once more ascend the throne from which the shameless, brazen goddess of power and wealth has driven them away—then this man we knew and loved will find his right-ful place in the minds and hearts of the cruel, unwilling world he served. No purer patriot ever lived than the friend we lay at rest today. His love of country was not paraded in the public marts, or bartered in the stalls for gold; his patriotism was of that pure ideal mold that placed love of man about the love of self.

John P. Altgeld was always and at all times a lover of his fellow-man. Those who reviled him have tried to teach the world that he was bitter and relentless, that he hated more than loved. We who knew the man, we who clasped his hand and heard his voice and looked into his smiling face; we who knew his life of kindness, of charity, of infinite pity to the outcast and the weak; we who knew his human heart, could never be deceived. A truer, greater, gentler, kindlier soul has never lived and died; and the fierce bitterness and hatred that sought to destroy this great, grand soul had but one cause—the fact that he really loved his fellow-man.

As a youth our dead chieftain risked his life for the cause of the black man, whom he always loved. As a lawyer he was wise

and learned, impatient with the forms and machinery which
courts and legislators and lawyers have woven to strangle justice
through expense and ceremony and delay; as a judge he found
a legal way to do what seemed right to him, and if he could not
find a legal way, he found away. As a governor of a great
state, he ruled wisely and well. Elected by the greatest personal
triumph of any governor chosen by the state, he fearlessly and
knowingly bared his devoted head to the fiercest, most vindictive
criticism ever heaped upon a public man, because he loved justice and dared to do the right.

In the days now past, John P. Altgeld, our loving chief, in
scorn and derision was called John Pardon Altgeld by those who
would destroy his power. We who stand today around his bier
and mourn the brave and loving friend are glad to adopt this
name. If, in the infinite economy of nature, there shall be another land where crooked paths shall be made straight, where
heaven's justice shall review the judgments of the earth—if there
shall be a great, wise, humane judge, before whom the sons of
men shall come, we can hope for nothing better for ourselves
than to pass into that infinite presence as the comrades and
friends of John Pardon Altgeld, who opened the prison doors
and set the captive free.

Even admirers have seldom understood the real character of
this great human man. These were sometimes wont to feel that
the fierce bitterness of the world that assailed him fell on deaf
ears and an unresponsive soul. They did not know the man, and
they do not feel the subtleties of human life. It was not a callous
heart that so often led him to brave the most violent and malicious hate; it was not a callous heart, it was a devoted soul. He
so loved justice and truth and liberty and righteousness that all
the terrors that the earth could hold were less than the condemnation of his own conscience for an act that was cowardly
or mean.

John P. Altgeld, like many of the earth's greatest souls, was a
solitary man. Life to him was serious and earnest—an endless
tragedy. The earth was a great hospital of sick, wounded and
suffering, and he a devoted surgeon, who had no right to waste
one moment's time and whose duty was to cure them all. While
he loved his friends, he yet could work without them, he could

live without them, he could bid them one by one goodbye, when their courage failed to follow where he led; and he could go alone, out into the silent night, and, looking upward at the changeless stars, could find communion there.

My dear, dead friend, long and well have we known you, devotedly have we followed you, implicitly have we trusted you, fondly have we loved you. Beside your bier we now must say farewell. The heartless call has come, and we must stagger on the best we can alone. In the darkest hours we will look in vain for your loved form, we will listen hopelessly for your devoted, fearless voice. But, though we lay you in the grave and hide you from the sight of man, your brave words will speak for the poor, the oppressed, the captive and the weak; and your devoted life inspire countless souls to do and dare in the holy cause for which you lived and died.